Better Homes and Gardens.

tasty
chicken
dinners

Better Homes and Gardens®

tasty chicken dinners

WILEY

John Wiley & Sons, Inc.

John Wiley & Sons, Inc.
Publisher: Natalie Chapman
Associate Publisher: Jessica Goodman
Executive Editor: Anne Ficklen
Production Manager: Michael Olivo
Production Editor: Abby Saul
Cover Design: Suzanne Sunwoo
Art Director: Tai Blanche
Layout: Indianapolis Composition
  Services
Manufacturing Manager: Tom Hyland

Test Kitchen

Our seal assures you that every recipe in *Tasty Chicken Dinners* has been tested in the Better Homes and Gardens® Test Kitchen. This means that each recipe is practical and reliable and meets our high standards of taste appeal. We guarantee your satisfaction with this book for as long as you own it.

This book is printed on acid-free paper.

For general information on our other products and services or for technical support, please contact our Customer Care Department within the United States at (877) 762–2974, outside the United States at (317) 572–3993 or fax (317) 572–4002.

Wiley also publishes its books in a variety of electronic formats. Some content that appears in print may not be available in electronic books. For more information about Wiley products, visit our web site at www.wiley.com.

Library of Congress Cataloging-in-Publication Data is available upon request.

ISBN: 978-1-435-12635-0

Printed in China.

10 9 8 7 6 5 4 3 2 1

contents

appetizers
AND SNACKS

**Buffalo Chicken Drumsticks
with Blue Cheese Dip,** *page 13*

mandarin APRICOT CHICKEN WINGS

Prep: 15 minutes
Bake: 25 minutes
Oven: 400°F
Makes: 8 servings

2 pounds chicken wing drummettes (about 16)

⅔ cup bottled sweet-and-sour sauce

½ cup snipped dried apricots

⅓ cup bottled hoisin sauce

¼ cup soy sauce

2 tablespoons honey

2 cloves garlic, minced

¼ teaspoon ground ginger

¼ teaspoon five-spice powder

1 tablespoon sesame seeds, toasted

Scallions (optional)

Dried apricot halves (optional)

1 Preheat oven to 400°F. Arrange drummettes in a single layer in a baking pan or roasting pan lined with foil. Bake drummettes for 20 minutes.

2 Meanwhile, in a small saucepan, stir together sweet-and-sour sauce, the snipped apricots, the hoisin sauce, soy sauce, honey, garlic, ginger, and five-spice powder. Bring to boiling; reduce the heat. Simmer, uncovered, for 5 minutes. Remove from the heat.

3 Brush about ¼ cup of the sauce mixture over drummettes. Sprinkle with sesame seeds. Bake for about 5 minutes more or until drummettes are no longer pink in the center. Serve drummettes with remaining sauce. If desired, garnish with scallion and serve with dried apricot halves.

Nutrition facts per serving: 129 cal., 8 g total fat (2 g sat. fat), 44 mg chol., 411 mg sodium, 11 g carb., 0 g dietary fiber, 8 g protein.

Make-Ahead Directions: Prepare sauce as directed; cool. Cover and chill for up to 24 hours before using.

wings, TWO WAYS

Our options are hot and spicy or sweet and tangy—two kinds of wings for all kinds of people. Most will love both!

Prep: 10 minutes
Bake: 1 hour
Broil: 16 minutes per batch
Oven: 425°F/broil
Makes: 70 wings

1 package (5 pounds) frozen chicken wingettes or 5 pounds chicken wings, each cut into 2 pieces (70 pieces total)

Buffalo Sauce

¾ cup hot pepper sauce
4 tablespoons unsalted butter, melted

Maple BBQ Sauce

1 cup ketchup
½ cup maple syrup
6 tablespoons cider vinegar

For serving

3 scallions
4 ribs celery, cut in 4-inch sticks
Thick blue cheese dressing (optional)

1 Preheat oven to 425°F. Place wing pieces in large deep roasting pan—no need to thaw. Bake for 1 hour or until cooked through and meat begins to pull away from the ends, stirring frequently. Remove pan to a wire rack. Using tongs, divide wing pieces between two 15x10-inch jelly-roll pans, shaking excess fat back into roasting pan.

2 Heat oven to broil. Stir together ingredients for Buffalo Sauce; stir together ingredients for Maple BBQ Sauce. Brush enough Buffalo Sauce onto wing pieces in one pan to coat. Broil for about 7 minutes or until crispy. Remove, turn wing pieces over, brush with more sauce. Broil for 7 minutes longer. Remove and let cool briefly on wire rack. Repeat with Maple BBQ Sauce on wings in second pan, broiling each side for 8 minutes. Remove and let cool briefly. Reserve any leftover Maple BBQ Sauce. Serve immediately or cover when completely cool and refrigerate for up to 1 day.

3 To serve, uncover and reheat if necessary at 350°F for about 20 minutes or until hot, turning occasionally. Place on platter with scallions and celery. If desired, serve with blue cheese dressing and reserved Maple BBQ Sauce (boiled for 3 minutes).

Nutrition facts per wing with Buffalo Sauce: 76 cal., 6 g total fat (2 g sat. fat), 26 mg chol., 122 mg sodium, 0 g carb., 0 g dietary fiber, 5 g protein.
Nutrition facts per wing with Maple BBQ Sauce: 76 calories, 5 g fat (1 g sat.), 26 mg chol., 144 mg sodium, 3 g carb., 0 g dietary fiber, 5 g protein.

maple-glazed APPLE-CHICKEN SAUSAGE BITES

Prep: 10 minutes
Bake: 16 minutes
Oven: 375°F
Makes: 12 appetizers

1 **12- to 16-ounce package cooked apple-flavor chicken sausage links**

⅓ **cup maple syrup**

1 **tablespoon stone-ground mustard**

2 **teaspoons snipped fresh sage, or ½ teaspoon dried sage, crushed**

16 **to 20 pretzel sticks**

1 Preheat oven to 375°F. Cut sausage into 1-inch slices. Place in a shallow baking pan. For maple glaze, in a small bowl combine maple syrup, mustard, and sage.

2 Bake sausage for 8 minutes. Brush generously with maple glaze. Bake about 8 minutes more or until sausage is glazed and thoroughly heated through, stirring once.

3 Use pretzel sticks as edible toothpicks to serve sausage slices.

Nutrition facts per appetizer: 68 cal., 2 g total fat (1 g sat. fat), 22 mg chol., 185 mg sodium, 8 g carb., 0 g dietary fiber, 5 g protein.

buffalo CHICKEN DRUMSTICKS WITH BLUE CHEESE DIP

Prep: 30 minutes
Cook: 6 to 8 hours (low)
    or 3 to 4 hours
    (high)
Makes: 8 servings

16 chicken drumsticks (about
    4 pounds), skinned, if
    desired

1 16-ounce bottle buffalo
    wing hot sauce (2 cups)

¼ cup tomato paste

2 tablespoons white or
    cider vinegar

2 tablespoons
    Worcestershire sauce

1 8-ounce container sour
    cream

½ cup mayonnaise or salad
    dressing

½ cup crumbled blue cheese
    (2 ounces)

¼ to ½ teaspoon cayenne
    pepper or bottled hot
    pepper sauce

    Celery sticks

1 Place drumsticks in a 4- to 5-quart slow cooker. In a medium bowl, combine hot sauce, tomato paste, vinegar, and Worcestershire sauce. Pour over chicken in cooker.

2 Cover and cook on low-heat setting for 6 to 8 hours or on high-heat setting for 3 to 4 hours.

3 Meanwhile, for blue cheese dip, in a small bowl combine sour cream, mayonnaise, blue cheese, and cayenne pepper. Cover and chill the dip until ready to serve.

4 Using a slotted spoon, remove drumsticks from cooker. Skim fat from cooking juices. Serve drumsticks with cooking juices, the blue cheese dip, and celery sticks.

Nutrition facts per serving: 454 cal., 33 g total fat (11 g sat. fat), 141 mg chol., 2084 mg sodium, 6 g carb., 1 g dietary fiber, 31 g protein.

mojo chicken wings
WITH MANGO SAUCE

Prep: 20 minutes
Marinate: 2 hours
Bake: 25 minutes
Oven: 450°F
Makes: 12 servings

1 cup mango nectar

½ cup lemon juice
  (3 lemons)

½ cup orange juice
  (2 oranges)

½ cup snipped fresh parsley

¼ cup red wine vinegar

¼ cup olive oil

6 cloves garlic, minced

1 or 2 fresh jalapeño chile
  peppers, seeded and
  finely chopped*

1 teaspoon salt

½ teaspoon ground cumin

24 chicken drumettes**
  (about 2½ pounds)

1 mango, peeled, pitted,
  and chopped

⅓ cup chopped onion
  (1 small)

¼ cup snipped fresh cilantro

1 For marinade, in a medium bowl whisk together mango nectar, lemon juice, orange juice, parsley, vinegar, oil, garlic, jalapeño pepper, salt, and cumin. Reserve ½ cup of the marinade for sauce; cover and chill until needed.

2 Place drumettes in a resealable plastic bag set in a shallow dish. Pour remaining marinade over drumettes; seal bag. Marinate in the refrigerator for 2 hours or overnight, turning bag occasionally. Drain chicken, discarding marinade.

3 Preheat oven to 450°F. Arrange drumettes in a single layer in a foil-lined 15x10x1-inch baking pan. Bake for about 25 minutes or until chicken is tender and no longer pink.

4 Meanwhile, for sauce, in a blender combine the reserved marinade with mango, onion, and cilantro. Cover and blend until smooth. Serve drumettes with sauce.

Nutrition facts per serving: 278 cal., 20 g fat (4 g sat. fat), 97 mg chol., 283 mg sodium, 9 g carb., 1 g dietary fiber, 17 g protein.

*Tip: Because hot chile peppers, such as jalapeños, contain volatile oils that can burn your skin and eyes, avoid direct contact with chiles as much as possible. When working with chile peppers, wear plastic or rubber gloves. If your bare hands do touch the chile peppers, wash your hands well with soap and water.

**Tip: If you cannot find chicken drumettes, use 12 chicken wings. Cut off and discard tips of chicken wings. Cut wings at joints to form 24 pieces.

CHICKEN-AND-RAISIN-STUFFED
mushrooms

Prep: 30 minutes
Bake: 13 minutes
Oven: 425°F
Makes: 15 appetizers

15 **large fresh mushrooms (2½ to 3 inches in diameter)**

3 **tablespoons butter**

¼ **cup thinly sliced scallions (2)**

1 **clove garlic, minced**

¾ **cup finely chopped cooked chicken or turkey (about 4 ounces)**

2 **tablespoons fine dry bread crumbs**

2 **tablespoons grated Parmesan cheese**

2 **tablespoons finely chopped smoke-flavor almonds**

2 **tablespoons chopped golden raisins**

1 **tablespoon snipped fresh parsley**

Olive oil

1 Preheat oven to 425°F. If desired, remove and discard stems from mushrooms. Set mushroom caps aside.

2 For filling, in a small saucepan melt butter over medium heat. Add scallions and garlic; cook and stir for about 2 minutes or until tender. Remove from heat. Stir in chicken, bread crumbs, cheese, almonds, raisins, and parsley.

3 Place mushrooms, stemmed sides down, in a 15x10x1-inch baking pan (if using mushrooms with stems intact, place stem sides up and omit the turning step). Bake for 5 minutes. Turn mushrooms stemmed sides up. Brush mushrooms with oil. Divide filling among mushrooms. Bake for 8 to 10 minutes more or until heated through.

Nutrition facts per appetizer: 60 cal., 4 g total fat (2 g sat. fat), 13 mg chol., 65 mg sodium, 3 g carb., 0 g dietary fiber, 3 g protein.

quick mexican LAYERED DIP

Prep: 20 minutes
Chill: 30 minutes
Makes: 10 to 12 servings

1 16-ounce can refried beans with green chile peppers

⅔ cup bottled ranch salad dressing

2 teaspoons taco seasoning

1½ cups finely chopped cooked chicken

1 cup purchased guacamole

1 large tomato, seeded and chopped

½ of a 2.25-ounce can sliced pitted black olives, drained (¼ cup)

Tortilla chips

1 Spread refried beans on a 12-inch round serving plate. In a small bowl, combine ranch salad dressing and taco seasoning; stir in chicken. Spoon on top of the beans in an even layer. Spoon guacamole in small mounds on top of the chicken mixture. Carefully spread to an even layer.

2 Cover and chill for at least 30 minutes or up to 6 hours. Top with tomato and olives just before serving. Serve with tortilla chips.

Nutrition facts per serving: 206 cal., 14 g total fat (2 g sat. fat), 22 mg chol., 469 mg sodium, 11 g carb., 4 g dietary fiber, 9 g protein.

spicy CHICKEN-BEAN DIP

Prep: 15 minutes
Cook: 2½ hours to 3 hours (low)
Makes: 26 (¼-cup) servings

2 **8-ounce tubs cream cheese with chive and onion**

1 **10-ounce can chopped tomatoes and green chile peppers, undrained**

¼ **cup milk**

1 **teaspoon ground cumin**

½ **teaspoon fajita seasoning**

2 **cups finely chopped cooked chicken**

2 **cups shredded American cheese (8 ounces)**

2 **cups shredded Monterey Jack cheese (8 ounces)**

1 **15-ounce can white kidney (cannellini) or small white beans, rinsed and drained**

2 **tablespoons snipped fresh cilantro**

Pita wedges, toasted, and/or tortilla chips

1 In a 3½- or 4-quart slow cooker, combine cream cheese, tomatoes, milk, cumin, and fajita seasoning. Stir in chicken, American cheese, Monterey Jack cheese, and kidney beans.

2 Cover and cook on low-heat setting for 2½ to 3 hours. Serve immediately or keep covered on warm or low-heat setting for up to 2 hours. Just before serving, stir in cilantro. Serve dip with toasted pita wedges.

Nutrition facts per serving (dip only): 153 cal., 11 g total fat (7 g sat. fat), 39 mg chol., 324 mg sodium, 5 g carb., 1 g dietary fiber, 8 g protein.

picadillo CHICKEN PIZZETTAS

Sweet dried fruit, spicy salsa, and salty olives make this an out-of-the-ordinary pizza-style appetizer.

Prep: 25 minutes
Bake: 20 minutes
Oven: 425°F
Makes: 24 servings

1 6- or 6.5-ounce package pizza crust mix

1 cup bottled salsa

¼ teaspoon ground cinnamon

¼ teaspoon ground cumin

2 cups sliced or chopped cooked chicken

½ cup dried cranberries or raisins

½ cup pitted green olives, coarsely chopped

¼ cup sliced scallions or chopped onion

1 tablespoon sliced almonds

4 ounces shredded Manchego or Monterey Jack cheese (1 cup)

1 tablespoon snipped fresh cilantro

1 Preheat oven to 425°F. Prepare pizza crust according to package directions. Pat dough into a greased 15x10x1-inch baking pan (crust will be thin). Bake for 5 minutes.

2 In a small bowl, combine salsa, cinnamon, and cumin; spread evenly over crust. Top with chicken, cranberries, olives, scallions, and almonds. Sprinkle with cheese.

3 Bake for 15 minutes or until edges of crust are golden. Remove from oven; sprinkle with cilantro. Cut into 12 pieces; cut each piece in half diagonally.

Nutrition facts per serving: 87 cal., 4 g total fat (1 g sat. fat), 15 mg chol., 226 mg sodium, 8 g carb., 1 g dietary fiber, 6 g protein.

chicken-pesto TRIANGLES

If you don't have any leftover cooked chicken, stop by the supermarket deli counter and pick up a whole roasted chicken. It yields about 2 cups of cooked chicken. Freeze half of the chicken for another time.

Prep: 30 minutes
Bake: 15 minutes
Oven: 400°F
Makes: 16 appetizers

1 **15-ounce package folded refrigerated unbaked piecrust (2 crusts)**

1 **cup diced cooked chicken (5 ounces)**

¼ **cup slivered almonds or pine nuts, toasted and coarsely chopped**

⅓ **cup purchased pesto**

2 **tablespoons butter or margarine, melted**

1 **tablespoon sesame seeds or snipped fresh parsley**

1 Let piecrusts stand at room temperature according to package directions. Preheat oven to 400°F.

2 For filling, in a small bowl stir together chicken and nuts. Add pesto; toss until moistened.

3 Unfold one piecrust on a lightly floured surface; press flat with fingers. Cut piecrust into 8 wedges. Spoon 1 tablespoon of the filling onto the center of each pastry wedge near rounded edge. Brush edges with water. Fold the pointed end of the dough over filling. Fold sides over filling, pressing gently to seal. Place each filled triangle on an ungreased baking sheet. Brush with melted butter; sprinkle with sesame seeds or parsley. Repeat with remaining piecrust and filling.

4 Bake for 15 to 18 minutes or until pastry is golden. Serve warm.

Nutrition facts per appetizer: 193 cal., 13 g total fat (4 g sat. fat), 14 mg chol., 180 mg sodium, 14 g carb., 0 g dietary fiber, 4 g protein.

roasted PEPPER AND ARTICHOKE PIZZA

Prep: 25 minutes
Bake: 13 minutes
Oven: 425°F
Makes: 4 servings

1 12-inch whole wheat
   bread shell

½ cup pizza sauce

1 cup coarsely chopped or
   shredded cooked chicken
   breast (about 6 ounces)

½ of a 14-ounce can
   artichoke hearts, drained
   and coarsely chopped

1 cup bottled roasted red
   sweet peppers, drained
   and cut into strips

¼ cup sliced scallions or
   chopped red onion

¾ cup shredded reduced-fat
   mozzarella cheese
   (3 ounces)

2 ounces semisoft goat
   cheese, crumbled

1️⃣ Preheat oven to 425°F. Place bread shell on a large baking sheet.

2️⃣ Spread pizza sauce evenly on crust. Top with chicken, artichokes, roasted red peppers, and scallions. Top with mozzarella cheese and goat cheese.

3️⃣ Bake for 13 to 15 minutes or until toppings are hot and cheese is melted. Cut into quarters.

Nutrition facts per serving: 383 cal., 12 g total fat (6 g sat. fat), 52 mg chol., 935 mg sodium, 43 g carb., 8 g dietary fiber, 28 g protein.

endive SATAY BITES

Start to Finish: 30 minutes
Makes: about 30
      appetizers

1 **2- to 2½-pound purchased roasted chicken**

⅔ **cup peanut sauce**

¼ **cup honey-roasted peanuts, chopped**

¼ **cup snipped fresh cilantro**

2 **tablespoons lime juice**

1 **tablespoon packed brown sugar**

3 **to 4 heads Belgian endive, separated into leaves (about 30)**

    Snipped fresh cilantro (optional)

1 Remove and discard skin and bones from chicken; chop chicken (you should have about 3 cups).

2 In a large bowl, combine peanut sauce, peanuts, ¼ cup cilantro, lime juice, and brown sugar. Stir in chicken. Spoon mixture onto endive leaves. If desired, garnish with additional cilantro.

Nutrition facts per appetizer: 77 cal., 5 g total fat (1 g sat. fat), 27 mg chol., 310 mg sodium, 3 g carb., 0 g dietary fiber, 6 g protein.

philly CHICKEN-CHEESE SANDWICHES

Prep: 30 minutes
Cook: 3 minutes
Makes: 16 servings

1 tablespoon olive oil

12 ounces skinless, boneless chicken breast, cut into thin bite-size strips

¼ teaspoon salt

¼ teaspoon ground black pepper

1 medium red sweet pepper, cut into thin strips

1 medium yellow sweet pepper, cut into thin strips

1 medium onion, thinly sliced

2 cloves garlic, minced

½ teaspoon bottled hot pepper sauce

1 loaf Italian bread, split horizontally

¼ cup purchased basil pesto

4 ounces sliced provolone cheese

1 In a large skillet, heat oil over medium heat. Add chicken; sprinkle with salt and black pepper. Cook and stir for about 5 minutes or until chicken is no longer pink. Using a slotted spoon, remove from skillet.

2 Add sweet peppers, onion, and garlic to skillet. Cook and stir for 5 to 6 minutes or until tender. Stir in chicken and hot pepper sauce. Remove from heat.

3 Spread cut sides of Italian bread with pesto. Place chicken mixture and cheese on the bottom of loaf. Add the top of loaf and gently press together. Cut sandwich diagonally into 4 portions.

4 Preheat an electric sandwich press, a covered indoor grill, a large grill pan, or a large skillet. Place sandwich portions in the sandwich press or indoor grill; close lid. Cook for 3 to 4 minutes or until bread is toasted and cheese is melted. (If using a grill pan or skillet, place sandwich portions in grill pan or skillet. Weight down with a heavy skillet. Cook over medium heat for 3 to 4 minutes or until bread is toasted. Turn sandwich portions over, weight down, and cook for 3 to 4 minutes more or until bread is toasted and cheese is melted.)

5 Cut each sandwich portion diagonally into 4 slices; secure with toothpicks, if necessary.

Nutrition facts per serving: 192 cal., 8 g total fat (2 g sat. fat), 18 mg chol., 313 mg sodium, 21 g carb., 1 g dietary fiber, 10 g protein.

chipotle CHICKEN QUESADILLAS

Prep: 30 minutes
Cook: 2 minutes per batch
Oven: 300°F
Makes: 4 servings

- 8 7-inch whole wheat tortillas

  Nonstick cooking spray

- 12 ounces skinless, boneless chicken breast halves, cut into thin bite-size strips

- 2 small red and/or green sweet peppers, seeded and chopped

- 2 cloves garlic, minced

- ¼ cup thinly sliced scallions

- 1 canned chipotle chile pepper in adobo sauce, drained and finely chopped*

- 2 tablespoons lime juice

- 3 ounces queso fresco, crumbled, or ¾ cup shredded reduced-fat Monterey Jack cheese (3 ounces)

- ¼ cup light sour cream (optional)

- 1 teaspoon finely chopped canned chipotle chile pepper in adobo sauce*(optional)

- 4 cups shredded lettuce

  Purchased salsa and/or lime wedges (optional)

1 Preheat oven to 300°F. Lightly coat one side of each tortilla with nonstick cooking spray. Place tortillas, coated sides down, on a tray or clean work surface. Set aside.

2 Coat an unheated large nonstick skillet with nonstick cooking spray. Preheat skillet over medium-high heat. Add chicken, sweet peppers, and garlic to hot skillet. Cook for 4 to 6 minutes or until chicken is no longer pink, stirring occasionally. Remove from heat; stir in scallions, the one chipotle pepper, and the lime juice.

3 Divide chicken and pepper mixture among tortillas, placing the mixture on one half of each tortilla. Sprinkle chicken mixture with cheese. Fold tortillas over filling; press down lightly.

4 Heat a nonstick skillet or griddle over medium-high heat; reduce heat to medium. Cook quesadillas, 2 or 3 at a time, for 2 to 3 minutes or until tortilla is lightly browned, turning once halfway through cooking. Keep quesadillas warm in the oven while cooking the remaining quesadillas.

5 If desired, in a small bowl stir together sour cream and the 1 teaspoon chipotle pepper. Cut each quesadilla into 3 wedges. Serve with lettuce. If desired, serve with sour cream mixture, salsa, and/or lime wedges.

Nutrition facts per serving: 262 cal., 7 g total fat (0 g sat. fat), 49 mg chol., 440 mg sodium, 30 g carb., 18 g dietary fiber, 36 g protein.

*Tip: Because chile peppers contain volatile oils that can burn your skin and eyes, avoid direct contact with them as much as possible. When working with chile peppers, wear plastic or rubber gloves. If your bare hands do touch the peppers, wash your hands and nails well with soap and warm water.

thai-spiced CHICKEN AND PINEAPPLE

Prep: 30 minutes
Grill: 12 minutes
Makes: 4 servings

⅔ **cup bottled sweet-and-sour sauce***

2 **tablespoons snipped fresh Thai basil or sweet basil**

1 **teaspoon Thai seasoning or five-spice powder**

½ **teaspoon bottled minced garlic (1 clove)**

1 **tablespoon butter, melted**

1 **tablespoon packed brown sugar (optional)**

1 **small fresh pineapple**

Nonstick cooking spray or cooking oil

1 **pound skinless, boneless chicken breast halves, cut into 1-inch pieces**

Hot cooked rice (optional)

Thai basil or sweet basil sprigs (optional)

Whole fresh red chile peppers (optional)

1 For Thai sauce, in a small bowl combine sweet-and-sour sauce, the snipped basil, the Thai seasoning, and garlic. Transfer ¼ cup of the sauce to another bowl to brush onto chicken while grilling. Stir butter and, if desired, brown sugar into remaining sauce; cover and set aside.

2 Cut ends off of pineapple, exposing the flesh. Halve pineapple lengthwise; cut each half crosswise into 4 slices. Lightly coat pineapple slices with nonstick cooking spray or brush with oil. Set aside.

3 Thread chicken pieces onto four 10- to 12-inch metal skewers.

4 Place skewers on the grill rack directly over medium heat; grill for 12 to 14 minutes or until chicken is no longer pink, turning skewers once and brushing with the ¼ cup Thai sauce during the first 7 minutes of grilling. Discard remainder of Thai sauce used as a brush-on. While chicken is grilling, arrange pineapple slices on the grill rack directly over medium heat. Grill for 6 to 8 minutes or until heated through, turning once.

5 Serve chicken and pineapple with reserved Thai sauce and, if desired, rice. If desired, garnish with basil sprigs and chile peppers.

Nutrition facts per serving: 285 cal., 5 g total fat (2 g sat. fat), 73 mg chol., 332 mg sodium, 34 g carb., 2 g dietary fiber, 27 g protein.

***Tip:** Bottled sweet-and-sour sauces vary in sweetness and thickness. If you use a less sweet sauce, add the brown sugar to the Thai sauce. If you use a thick sweet-and-sour sauce, adjust the consistency of the finished Thai sauce by adding a little water.

buffalo-style CHICKEN FINGERS

Since the first spicy wings flew from Buffalo to parties across the country, countless variations have appeared. This neat-to-eat chicken breast version is a favorite.

Prep: 25 minutes
Bake: 18 minutes
Oven: 425°F
Makes: 12 servings

- 2 **cups crushed cornflakes**
- 2 **tablespoons finely snipped fresh parsley**
- ½ **teaspoon salt**
- 1 **pound skinless, boneless chicken breast halves**
- ⅓ **cup bottled blue cheese salad dressing**
- 2 **teaspoons water**
- 1 **to 2 teaspoons bottled hot pepper sauce**
  Celery sticks
  Bottled blue cheese salad dressing

1 Preheat oven to 425°F. In a shallow bowl or pie plate, combine crushed cornflakes, parsley, and salt. Cut chicken breasts into strips about ¾ inch wide and 3 inches long. In a large mixing bowl, combine ⅓ cup dressing, water, and hot pepper sauce. Add chicken; stir to coat. Roll chicken pieces individually in crumb mixture to coat.

2 Place chicken strips in a single layer on a lightly greased 15x10x1-inch baking pan. Bake for 18 to 20 minutes or until chicken is no longer pink and crumbs are golden. Serve warm with celery sticks and additional blue cheese dressing for dipping.

Nutrition facts per serving: 184 cal., 12 g total fat (2 g sat. fat), 26 mg chol., 408 mg sodium, 9 g carb., 0 g dietary fiber, 11 g protein.

Make-Ahead Directions: Prepare as directed through Step 1. Place coated chicken strips on a foil-lined baking sheet. Freeze for about 2 hours or until firm. Place frozen strips in a freezer container; cover. Freeze for up to 1 month. To serve, bake as directed in Step 2.

asian CHICKEN LETTUCE WRAPS

Start to Finish: 20 minutes
Makes: 4 (2-wrap) servings

- 3 **scallions**
- ½ **of a 6-ounce package refrigerated cooked chicken breast strips**
- ½ **of a medium green sweet pepper, seeded and cut up**
- 3 **tablespoons rice vinegar**
- 1 **teaspoon sesame oil or olive oil**
- ¼ **to ½ teaspoon ground black pepper**
- ¼ **teaspoon crushed red pepper (optional)**
- 1 **cup shredded cabbage**
- 2 **tablespoons water**
- 2 **tablespoons reduced-sodium soy sauce**
- 8 **leaves butterhead (Boston or Bibb) lettuce (about 1 small head)**

1 Trim off and discard root ends of scallions. Cut off and slice green tops and set aside. In a food processor, combine white parts of the scallions, the chicken breast, sweet pepper, 1 tablespoon of the vinegar, the oil, black pepper, and, if desired, crushed red pepper. Cover and pulse with several on-off turns until chicken mixture is finely chopped. Transfer to a medium microwave-safe bowl. Add cabbage and toss to combine; set aside.

2 For the dipping sauce, in a small bowl combine sliced scallion tops, the remaining 2 tablespoons vinegar, the water, and soy sauce.

3 Cover bowl of chicken mixture with vented plastic wrap. Microwave on 100% power (high) for 1 to 2 minutes or until heated through, stirring once halfway through cooking. Spoon a rounded 2 tablespoons of the chicken mixture on each lettuce leaf. Roll up and, if desired, cut in half. Serve with dipping sauce.

Nutrition facts per serving: 58 cal., 1 g total fat (0 g sat. fat), 11 mg chol., 333 mg sodium, 4 g carb., 1 g dietary fiber, 7 g protein.

Make-Ahead Directions: Prepare as above through Step 2. Transfer chicken mixture to a small microwave-safe storage container; cover and chill for up to 8 hours. Transfer dipping sauce to a small storage container; cover and chill until serving time. Serve as above in Step 3.

spicy MUSTARD STIR-FRY BITES

Prep: 25 minutes
Cook: 6 to 7 hours (low)
Makes: about 25
        appetizers

1 pound packaged chicken
   stir-fry strips

½ cup water

½ cup spicy brown mustard

4 teaspoons fajita
   seasoning

5 7- to 8-inch flour tortillas,
   warmed*

1 medium red, green, and/
   or yellow sweet pepper,
   seeded and cut into thin
   strips

   Snipped fresh cilantro
   and/or sliced scallion
   (optional)

1 Lightly coat a large skillet with cooking spray. Heat skillet over medium-high heat; add stir-fry strips. Cook and stir until brown. Drain off fat.

2 In a 1½-quart slow cooker, stir together the water, mustard, and fajita seasoning. Add stir-fry strips, stirring to coat.

3 Cover and cook on low-heat setting for 6 to 7 hours. Using a slotted spoon, transfer meat to a cutting board. Discard cooking liquid. Using two forks, pull meat apart into shreds.

4 Divide meat mixture evenly among the warmed tortillas. Top with sweet pepper strips and, if desired, cilantro and/or scallion. Roll up tortillas. Using a serrated knife, cut filled tortillas crosswise into bite-size pieces. If desired, skewer with decorative toothpicks.

Nutrition facts per appetizer: 60 cal., 2 g total fat (0 g sat. fat), 12 mg chol., 311 mg sodium, 6 g carb., 0 g dietary fiber, 5 g protein.

*Tip: To warm tortillas, stack tortillas and wrap tightly in foil. Heat in a 350°F oven for about 10 minutes or until heated through.

fried CHICKEN TENDERS

Prep: 35 minutes
Cook: 5 minutes per batch
Oven: 200°F
Makes: 10 to 12 servings

3 pounds fresh or frozen
   chicken breast
   tenderloins

Peanut oil or other
   vegetable oil for
   deep-fat frying

4 cups all-purpose flour

2 teaspoons garlic salt

1 teaspoon ground black
   pepper

3 cups buttermilk
   Cayenne-Butter Sauce*

Bottled blue cheese or
   ranch salad dressing, or
   Creamy Parmesan
   Dressing** (optional)

1 Thaw chicken, if frozen. In a deep-fat fryer or large deep saucepan, heat oil to 365°F.

2 Meanwhile, in a large bowl, stir together flour, garlic salt, and pepper; transfer half of the mixture to another bowl. Pour buttermilk into a medium bowl. Dip chicken into buttermilk, allowing excess to drip off. Dip into flour mixture, turning to coat. (When flour mixture in first bowl clumps too much, discard and use the flour mixture in second bowl.)

3 Fry chicken, one-quarter at a time, in hot oil for about 5 minutes or until coating is golden brown and chicken is no longer pink. Drain on paper towels. Keep warm on a baking sheet in a 200°F oven while frying the remaining chicken.

4 Serve chicken with Cayenne-Butter Sauce and, if desired, salad dressing.

*Cayenne-Butter Sauce: In a blender, combine 1 cup bottled cayenne pepper sauce and ⅔ cup melted butter. Cover and blend for about 1 minute or until slightly thickened. Makes about 1½ cups.

**Creamy Parmesan Dressing: In a small bowl, stir together ¾ cup mayonnaise or salad dressing; ¼ cup sour cream; 3 tablespoons grated Parmesan cheese; 2 teaspoons white wine vinegar or white vinegar; 1 clove garlic, minced; ½ teaspoon dried Italian seasoning, crushed; and, if desired, ¼ teaspoon ground black pepper. Makes about 1 cup.

Nutrition facts per serving: 648 cal., 35 g total fat (6 g sat. fat),
82 mg chol., 359 mg sodium, 42 g carb., 1 g dietary fiber, 39 g protein.

nutty CHICKEN FINGERS

When you're in the mood for chicken but time is of the essence, look to this Southern favorite. Pecans add a pleasing crunch to moist, tender chicken.

Prep: 10 minutes
Bake: 7 minutes
Oven: 400°F
Makes: 15 appetizers

- ⅓ **cup cornflake crumbs**
- ½ **cup finely chopped pecans**
- 1 **tablespoon dried parsley flakes**
- ⅛ **teaspoon salt**
- ⅛ **teaspoon garlic powder**
- 12 **ounces skinless, boneless chicken breast halves, cut into 3x1-inch strips**
- 2 **tablespoons skim milk**

1 Preheat oven to 400°F. In a shallow dish, combine cornflake crumbs, pecans, parsley, salt, and garlic powder. Dip chicken in milk, then roll in crumb mixture. Place in a 15x10x1-inch baking pan.

2 Bake for 7 to 9 minutes or until chicken is tender and no longer pink.

Nutrition facts per appetizer: 53 cal., 3 g total fat (0 g sat. fat), 12 mg chol., 42 mg sodium, 2 g carb., 0 g dietary fiber, 5 g protein.

rumaki

Prep: 15 minutes
Marinate: 4 to 24 hours
Broil: 8 minutes
Oven: broil
Makes: 24 to 28
      appetizers

**12 ounces chicken livers
(about 12 livers)**

¼ cup dry sherry

¼ cup soy sauce

2 tablespoons brown sugar

2 tablespoons cooking oil

¼ teaspoon garlic powder

⅛ teaspoon ground ginger

¼ cup water

**12 to 14 slices bacon, cut in
half crosswise**

**1 8-ounce can sliced water
chestnuts, drained**

1 Cut livers in half; quarter any extra-large livers. Place livers in a plastic bag set inside a deep bowl. Combine sherry, soy sauce, brown sugar, oil, garlic powder, ginger, and water; pour over livers. Marinate in the refrigerator for 4 to 24 hours, turning bag occasionally.

2 Preheat broiler. Drain livers. Wrap a bacon piece around a liver piece and water chestnut slice. Secure with a wooden toothpick. Place on a lightly greased broiler pan. Broil 4 inches from heat for 8 to 10 minutes or until livers are no longer pink, turning once. Serve warm.

Nutrition facts per appetizer: 53 cal., 3 g total fat (1 g sat. fat), 58 mg chol., 227 mg sodium, 2 g carb., 0 g dietary fiber, 3 g protein.

brandied PÂTÉ

Prep: 30 minutes
Chill: 8 to 24 hours
Cool: 1 hour
Bake: 1½ hours
Oven: 350°F
Makes: 32 servings

6 slices bacon

8 ounces chicken livers, drained and halved

1 large onion, cut up

2 eggs

½ cup brandy

4 cloves garlic

¼ cup all-purpose flour

2 teaspoons paprika

1 teaspoon dried rosemary, crushed

½ teaspoon salt

¼ teaspoon ground allspice

¼ teaspoon ground black pepper

1 pound ground pork

4 ounces ground cooked ham

2 bay leaves

Lettuce leaves (optional)

Fresh rosemary sprigs (optional)

Cherry tomatoes (optional)

Toasted baguette slices or crackers

1 Preheat oven to 350°F. In a large skillet, cook bacon until brown but still limp. Drain, reserving 2 tablespoons drippings in skillet. Drain bacon on paper towels; set aside.

2 Cook chicken livers in reserved drippings for about 5 minutes or until no longer pink. In food processor or blender, combine chicken livers, onion, eggs, brandy, garlic, flour, paprika, dried rosemary, salt, allspice, and pepper. Cover; blend or process until smooth. If using food processor, add pork and ham; cover and process until well mixed. (If using a blender, transfer mixture to a large bowl; add pork and ham and mix well.)

3 Lay the bacon slices crosswise to cover bottom and sides of an 8x4x2-inch loaf pan. Spoon meat mixture into pan; press firmly. Top with bay leaves. Cover pan tightly with foil. Place on a baking sheet. Bake for 1½ hours.

4 Remove foil; drain well. Place pan on a wire rack. Place several pieces of heavy foil directly on top of pâté; place weights on the foil. Cool for 1 hour at room temperature; chill for at least 8 hours or up to 24 hours with weights on top.

5 To serve, remove weights and foil. Remove bay leaves. Unmold pâté onto a serving plate. If desired, garnish with lettuce leaves, fresh rosemary, and cherry tomatoes. Thinly slice. Serve with baguette slices or crackers.

Nutrition facts per serving: 67 cal., 4 g total fat (1 g sat. fat), 48 mg chol., 122 mg sodium, 2 g carb., 0 g dietary fiber, 5 g protein.

salads

Chicken Tossed Salad, *page 42*

chicken TOSSED SALAD

This combination of garlic-pepper chicken and vegetables offers another easy salad option when you're in a hurry or craving cool, fresh flavors.

Start to Finish: 20 minutes
Makes: 4 servings

- 4 **skinless, boneless chicken breast halves (about 1¼ pounds total)**
- 1 **tablespoon extra-virgin olive oil**
- ¼ **teaspoon garlic-pepper seasoning**
- 8 **cups torn mixed salad greens**
- 1 **medium yellow or red sweet pepper, cut into bite-size strips**
- 1 **medium tomato, cut into wedges**
- ½ **cup bottled reduced-calorie berry or roasted garlic vinaigrette salad dressing**
- ¼ **cup crumbled feta cheese (1 ounce)**
- ¼ **cup whole wheat croutons (optional)**

1 Brush chicken breasts with olive oil; sprinkle with garlic-pepper seasoning. In a large nonstick skillet, cook chicken over medium heat for 8 to 10 minutes or until tender and no longer pink (170°F), turning once. Cut the chicken into bite-size strips.

2 In a large serving bowl, combine salad greens, sweet pepper, and tomato. Pour salad dressing over greens mixture; toss gently to coat. Top with chicken, feta cheese, and, if desired, croutons.

Nutrition facts per serving: 312 cal., 10 g total fat (2 g sat. fat), 88 mg chol., 217 mg sodium, 20 g carb., 2 g dietary fiber, 36 g protein.

balsamic CHICKEN OVER GREENS

Prep: 15 minutes
Marinate: 1 to 4 hours
Broil: 12 minutes
Oven: broil
Makes: 4 servings

 4 **skinless, boneless chicken breast halves (about 1 pound total)**

 ¾ **cup bottled reduced-calorie balsamic vinaigrette salad dressing**

 3 **cloves garlic, minced**

 ¼ **teaspoon crushed red pepper**

 8 **cups torn mixed salad greens**

1 Place chicken breast halves in a resealable plastic bag set in a shallow dish. For marinade, stir together ⅓ cup of the vinaigrette, the garlic, and crushed red pepper. Pour marinade over the chicken. Seal bag; turn to coat chicken. Marinate in the refrigerator for 1 to 4 hours, turning bag occasionally.

2 Preheat broiler. Drain chicken, reserving marinade. Place chicken on the unheated rack of a broiler pan. Broil 4 to 5 inches from heat for 12 to 15 minutes or until chicken is no longer pink (170°F), turning once and brushing with reserved marinade halfway through broiling. Discard any remaining marinade.

3 Divide greens among serving plates. Slice chicken. Place chicken on greens. Serve with the remaining vinaigrette.

Nutrition facts per serving: 203 cal., 7 g total fat (1 g sat. fat), 66 mg chol., 703 mg sodium, 6 g carb., 1 g dietary fiber, 28 g protein.

berry CHICKEN SALAD

Prep: 30 minutes
Marinate: 1 to 4 hours
Grill: 12 minutes
Makes: 4 servings

½ cup orange juice

¼ cup lime juice

¼ cup lemon juice

1 tablespoon olive oil

1 teaspoon chopped fresh basil

¾ teaspoon salt

½ teaspoon ground black pepper

4 skinless, boneless chicken breast halves (1¼ to 1½ pounds total)

3 cups fresh blackberries

¼ cup red wine vinegar

3 tablespoons sugar

1 teaspoon Dijon-style mustard

¼ teaspoon dried oregano, crushed

½ cup olive oil

1 8-ounce package Mediterranean mixed salad greens

2 medium pears, cored and thinly sliced

¾ cup crumbled feta cheese (3 ounces)

1 In a small bowl, combine orange juice, lime juice, lemon juice, the 1 tablespoon oil, basil, ½ teaspoon of the salt, and ¼ teaspoon of the pepper. Place chicken in a resealable plastic bag set in a shallow dish. Pour the juice mixture over chicken; seal bag. Marinate in the refrigerator for 1 to 4 hours, turning bag occasionally.

2 For dressing, in a blender, combine 1 cup of the blackberries, vinegar, sugar, mustard, oregano, and remaining ¼ teaspoon salt and ¼ teaspoon pepper. Cover and blend until smooth. With blender running, add the ½ cup oil in a thin, steady stream until well combined. Transfer dressing to serving container. Cover and chill until serving time.

3 Drain chicken, discarding marinade. For a charcoal grill, place chicken on the rack of an uncovered grill directly over medium coals. Grill for 12 to 15 minutes or until chicken is no longer pink (170°F), turning once halfway through grilling. (For a gas grill, preheat grill. Reduce heat to medium. Place chicken on grill rack over heat. Cover; grill as above.)

4 Slice chicken crosswise. Divide greens among dinner plates. Top with chicken, pears, and remaining 2 cups blackberries. Top each salad with some of the dressing and feta cheese. Pass remaining dressing.

Nutrition facts per serving: 603 cal., 35 g total fat (7 g sat. fat), 101 mg chol., 427 mg sodium, 36 g carb., 9 g dietary fiber, 38 g protein.

apple AND CHICKEN SALAD

Prep: 20 minutes
Grill: 12 minutes
Makes: 4 servings

⅓ **cup apple jelly**

3 **tablespoons horseradish mustard**

4 **skinless, boneless chicken breast halves (about 1 pound total)**

4 **cups mesclun or torn mixed salad greens**

2 **medium tart apples, cored and sliced**

¼ **cup coarsely chopped walnuts, toasted**

1 **tablespoon cider vinegar**

1 **tablespoon canola oil**

1 In a small saucepan, melt apple jelly over low heat. Remove from heat; stir in mustard. Set aside 2 tablespoons of the jelly mixture to brush on chicken. Reserve remaining jelly mixture for dressing.

2 For a charcoal grill, place chicken on the rack of an uncovered grill directly over medium coals. Grill for 12 to 15 minutes or until no longer pink (170°F), turning once halfway through grilling. (For a gas grill, preheat grill. Reduce heat to medium. Place chicken on grill rack over heat. Cover and grill as above.) Brush chicken with the 2 tablespoons jelly mixture. Transfer chicken to a cutting board; cool slightly and cut into bite-size pieces.

3 Meanwhile, in a large bowl toss together mesclun, apples, and walnuts. For dressing, whisk together the reserved jelly mixture, the cider vinegar, and oil. Divide greens mixture among serving plates. Arrange chicken on the greens; drizzle with the dressing.

Nutrition facts per serving: 330 cal., 10 g total fat (1 g sat. fat), 66 mg chol., 176 mg sodium, 32 g carb., 3 g dietary fiber, 29 g protein.

crispy CHOPPED CHICKEN SALAD

Prep: 45 minutes
Bake: 8 minutes
Cook: 8 minutes
Oven: 400°F
Makes: 6 servings

6   **thin slices prosciutto (about 4 ounces)**

½   **cup extra-virgin olive oil**

4   **skinless, boneless chicken breast halves**

Salt and ground black pepper

Paprika

2   **lemons**

1   **shallot, finely chopped**

2   **small carrots, peeled and thinly sliced**

2   **medium zucchini, chopped**

1   **medium red sweet pepper, chopped**

1   **medium yellow sweet pepper, chopped**

½   **of a small red onion, chopped**

5   **ounces blue cheese, crumbled**

Romaine lettuce leaves

1 Preheat oven to 400°F. Place prosciutto in single layer on large baking sheet. Bake until crisp, 8 to 10 minutes. Set aside.

2 In a large nonstick skillet, heat 1 tablespoon of oil over medium heat. Sprinkle chicken with salt, pepper, and paprika; add to skillet. Cook for 8 to 10 minutes or until chicken is no longer pink (170°F), turning once. Cool slightly; slice.

3 For lemon dressing, finely shred zest from one lemon; squeeze lemons to make ⅓ cup juice. In a small bowl, whisk together remaining olive oil, lemon juice, shredded zest, and shallot. Season with salt and pepper.

4 In a large bowl, combine carrots, zucchini, sweet peppers, onion, and chicken. Toss with dressing. Add blue cheese.

5 Line salad bowls with romaine. Spoon in chicken mixture. Top with prosciutto.

Nutrition facts per serving: 425 cal., 28 g total fat (8 g sat. fat), 86 mg chol., 965 mg sodium, 10 g carb., 2 g dietary fiber, 34 g protein.

mexican CHICKEN SALAD STACKS

If you're in a hurry, simply toss the ingredients together and serve this seasoned chicken medley in salad bowls.

Prep: 30 minutes
Broil: 6 minutes
Oven: broil
Makes: 4 servings

4 small skinless, boneless chicken breast halves (1 to 1¼ pounds total)

1 teaspoon ancho chile powder or chili powder

½ teaspoon dried oregano, crushed

½ teaspoon dried thyme, crushed

⅛ teaspoon salt

⅛ teaspoon ground black pepper

2 tablespoons orange juice

1 tablespoon olive oil

1 tablespoon white wine vinegar

1 teaspoon honey

4 cups shredded romaine lettuce

1 avocado, pitted, peeled, and sliced

2 oranges, peeled and sectioned

1 ounce queso fresco cheese, crumbled, or reduced-fat Monterey Jack cheese, shredded (¼ cup)

1 Place each chicken breast half between two pieces of plastic wrap. Using the flat side of a meat mallet, pound chicken until about ½ inch thick. Remove plastic wrap.

2 Preheat broiler. In a small bowl, stir together chile powder, oregano, thyme, salt, and black pepper. Sprinkle spice mixture evenly over chicken pieces; rub in with your fingers.

3 Place chicken on the unheated rack of a broiler pan. Broil 4 to 5 inches from the heat for 6 to 8 minutes or until chicken is tender and no longer pink (170°F), turning once halfway through broiling. Slice chicken.

4 Meanwhile, in a medium bowl, whisk together the orange juice, oil, vinegar, and honey. Add lettuce; toss to coat.

5 To assemble, divide lettuce mixture among dinner plates. Top with sliced chicken, avocado, and orange sections. Sprinkle with cheese.

Nutrition facts per serving: 306 cal., 13 g total fat (3 g sat. fat), 68 mg chol., 153 mg sodium, 18 g carb., 7 g dietary fiber, 30 g protein.

parisian CHICKEN SALAD

Prep: 25 minutes
Marinate: 6 to 8 hours
Broil: 12 minutes
Oven: broil
Makes: 4 servings

4 skinless, boneless chicken breast halves (1¼ to 1½ pounds total)

2 teaspoons finely shredded orange zest

⅓ cup orange juice

4 cloves garlic, minced

2 tablespoons honey

1½ teaspoons dried thyme, crushed

½ teaspoon salt

¼ teaspoon ground black pepper

¼ cup olive oil

2 tablespoons white wine vinegar

2 tablespoons orange juice

2 cloves garlic, minced

1½ teaspoons finely chopped shallot

4 cups torn baby salad greens

1 medium yellow or red sweet pepper, thinly sliced

2 medium oranges, peeled and sectioned

1 Place chicken in a resealable plastic bag set in a shallow dish. For marinade, combine orange zest, the ⅓ cup orange juice, the 4 cloves garlic, honey, and thyme. Pour over chicken; seal bag. Marinate in the refrigerator for 6 to 8 hours, turning bag occasionally.

2 Drain chicken, discarding marinade. Place chicken on the unheated rack of a broiler pan. Season with half of the salt and half of the pepper. Broil 4 to 5 inches from heat for 12 to 15 minutes or until chicken is no longer pink (170°F), turning once halfway through broiling.

3 Meanwhile, for dressing, in a screw-top jar combine olive oil, vinegar, the 2 tablespoons orange juice, the 2 cloves garlic, shallots, and remaining salt and pepper. Cover and shake well.

4 Divide greens among dinner plates. Top with sweet pepper slices. Slice chicken crosswise. Arrange chicken and orange sections over greens. Drizzle with dressing.

Nutrition facts per serving: 305 cal., 17 g total fat (3 g sat. fat), 59 mg chol., 261 mg sodium, 16 g carb., 1 g dietary fiber, 23 g protein.

mediterranean TABBOULEH SALAD WITH CHICKEN

Prep: 30 minutes
Chill: 4 to 24 hours
Stand: 30 minutes
Makes: 6 servings

1½ **cups water**

½ **cup bulgur**

2 **medium tomatoes, chopped**

1 **cup finely chopped seeded cucumber**

1 **cup finely chopped fresh flat-leaf parsley**

⅓ **cup thinly sliced scallions**

¼ **cup snipped fresh mint, or 1 tablespoon dried mint, crushed**

⅓ **to ½ cup lemon juice**

¼ **cup olive oil**

½ **teaspoon salt**

½ **teaspoon ground black pepper**

12 **large leaves romaine and/or butterhead (Bibb or Boston) lettuce**

18 **ounces grilled or broiled skinless, boneless chicken breast halves,* sliced**

1 In a large bowl, combine the water and bulgur. Let stand for 30 minutes. Drain bulgur through a fine sieve, using a large spoon to press out excess water. Return bulgur to bowl. Stir in tomatoes, cucumber, parsley, scallions, and mint.

2 For dressing, in a screw-top jar combine lemon juice, oil, salt, and pepper. Cover and shake well. Pour dressing over the bulgur mixture. Toss lightly to coat. Cover and chill for 4 to 24 hours, stirring occasionally. Bring to room temperature before serving.

3 Serve romaine with bulgur mixture and cooked chicken.

Nutrition facts per serving: 294 cal., 13 g total fat (2 g sat. fat), 72 mg chol., 276 mg sodium, 16 g carb., 5 g dietary fiber, 30 g protein.

*Tip: To grill chicken breast halves, lightly sprinkle chicken with salt and black pepper. For a charcoal grill, place chicken on the rack of an uncovered grill directly over medium coals. Grill for 12 to 15 minutes or until chicken is no longer pink (170°F), turning once halfway through grilling. (For a gas grill, preheat grill. Reduce heat to medium. Place chicken on grill rack over heat. Cover and grill as above.)

To broil chicken breast halves, preheat broiler. Lightly sprinkle chicken with salt and black pepper. Place chicken on the unheated rack of a broiler pan. Broil chicken 4 to 5 inches from heat for 12 to 15 minutes or until chicken is no longer pink (170°F), turning once halfway through broiling.

chicken, PEAR, AND BLUE CHEESE SALAD

The pairing of mellow pears and tangy blue cheese is naturally fresh and simple. Combine this classic twosome with packaged assorted greens and rotisserie chicken from the deli, and you've got a dinner that's naturally elegant as well.

Start to Finish: 15 minutes
Makes: 4 servings

1 **8-ounce package torn mixed salad greens or mesclun**

10 **to 12 ounces roasted or grilled boneless chicken breast, sliced**

¾ **cup reduced-calorie or regular blue cheese salad dressing**

2 **ripe pears, cored and sliced**

Ground black pepper (optional)

1 In a large bowl, combine salad greens, chicken, and salad dressing; toss gently to coat.

2 Divide greens mixture among salad bowls or dinner plates. Arrange pear slices on greens mixture. If desired, sprinkle with ground black pepper.

Nutrition facts per serving: 208 cal., 6 g total fat (2 g sat. fat), 72 mg chol., 591 mg sodium, 18 g carb., 3 g dietary fiber, 23 g protein.

thai COBB SALAD

Leftover grilled or deli-sliced meats work admirably in this refreshing salad. To carry through the Asian flavors, include Chinese cabbage as part of the greens mixture.

Start to Finish: 25 minutes
Makes: 4 servings

- ½ cup bottled Italian salad dressing
- 1 tablespoon soy sauce
- 1 to 1½ teaspoons grated fresh ginger
- ¼ to ½ teaspoon crushed red pepper
- 8 cups torn mixed salad greens
- 1½ cups coarsely chopped cooked chicken (8 ounces)
- 1 avocado, pitted, peeled, and cut into ½-inch pieces
- 1 cup coarsely shredded carrots
- ¼ cup fresh cilantro leaves
- ¼ cup thinly sliced scallions
- ¼ cup honey-roasted peanuts

1 For dressing, in a large bowl stir together salad dressing, soy sauce, ginger, and crushed red pepper. Add mixed salad greens; toss lightly to coat.

2 Divide salad greens among dinner plates. Top with chicken, avocado, carrots, cilantro, scallions, and peanuts.

Nutrition facts per serving: 255 cal., 15 g total fat (4 g sat. fat), 52 mg chol., 743 mg sodium, 11 g carb., 4 g dietary fiber, 19 g protein.

curried CHICKEN SALAD

Prep: 15 minutes
Chill: 1 hour
Cook: 8 minutes
Makes: 4 servings

2 skinless, boneless chicken breast halves (about 8 ounces)

Nonstick cooking spray

Pinch of onion powder

Pinch of garlic powder

1 Gala or Fuji apple, cored and chopped

½ cup chopped scallions

½ cup chopped celery

⅓ cup seedless golden raisins

¼ cup unsalted sliced almonds

Curried Salad Dressing*

8 Boston lettuce leaves

Unsalted sliced almonds (optional)**

① Heat a medium nonstick skillet over medium heat. Coat chicken with cooking spray. Sprinkle with onion powder and garlic powder. Cook for 4 to 5 minutes on each side or until no longer pink. Cool slightly; cut chicken into bite-size pieces.

② In a medium bowl, combine apple, scallion, and celery. Add the cooked chicken, raisins, and ¼ cup almonds. Spoon Curried Salad Dressing over the salad and stir to cover all. Cover and chill for 1 hour.

③ To serve, spoon ½ cup salad into each lettuce leaf and, if desired, sprinkle with additional almonds.

***Curried Salad Dressing:** Combine ½ cup light sour cream, 1 to 2 teaspoons curry powder, 1 teaspoon honey, ½ teaspoon ground ginger, and a pinch of cayenne pepper. Stir until smooth. Set aside in the refrigerator.

Nutrition facts per serving: 209 cal., 6 g total fat (2 g sat. fat), 41 mg chol., 69 mg sodium, 24 g carb., 3 g dietary fiber, 16 g protein.

****Tip:** Unsalted cashews may be substituted for the almonds.

stack-it-up CHICKEN SALAD

Start to Finish: 30 minutes
Makes: 4 servings

6 cups cut-up romaine or napa cabbage

2 cups chopped cooked chicken breast (about 10 ounces)

1 small apple, cored and cut into chunks

½ cup seedless green and/or red grapes, halved

3 tablespoons water

2 tablespoons reduced-fat peanut butter

2 teaspoons reduced-sodium soy sauce

¼ teaspoon ground ginger

1 On serving plates, stack romaine, chicken, apple, and grapes.

2 For dressing, in a small bowl whisk together the water, peanut butter, soy sauce, and ginger; drizzle over arranged salads.

Nutrition facts per serving: 205 cal., 6 g total fat (1 g sat. fat), 60 mg chol., 218 mg sodium, 14 g carb., 3 g dietary fiber, 25 g protein.

chicken AND PASTA SALAD

To save time and energy, roast two chickens at the same time; use one for dinner tonight, and refrigerate the other for this fruity salad in a day or two.

Prep: 30 minutes
Chill: 4 to 24 hours
Makes: 6 servings

1½ **cups dried radiatore, mostaccioli, or medium shell pasta**

3 **cups chopped cooked chicken**

3 **cups seedless red or green grapes, halved**

1½ **cups halved small strawberries**

1 **8-ounce can sliced water chestnuts, drained**

⅔ **cup bottled cucumber ranch salad dressing**

⅛ **teaspoon cayenne pepper**

1 **to 2 tablespoons milk (optional)**

Leaf lettuce

Sliced almonds, toasted (optional)

1 Cook pasta according to package directions; drain. Rinse with cold water; drain again.

2 In a large bowl, combine cooked pasta, chicken, grapes, strawberries, and water chestnuts.

3 For dressing, in a small bowl stir together bottled dressing and cayenne pepper. Pour dressing over pasta mixture; toss gently to coat. Cover and chill for 4 to 24 hours.

4 If necessary, stir enough of the milk into the pasta mixture to moisten. Line large salad plates with lettuce. Mound pasta mixture on top of lettuce. If desired, sprinkle with almonds.

Nutrition facts per serving: 447 cal., 19 g total fat (3 g sat. fat), 62 mg chol., 265 mg sodium, 44 g carb., 3 g dietary fiber, 25 g protein.

classic COBB SALAD

Hollywood's Brown Derby restaurant made this all-star salad famous. You'll find a combination of chopped chicken, avocado, eggs, crisp lettuce, bacon, creamy herb dressing, and tangy blue cheese in every bite.

Prep: 20 minutes
Cook: 15 minutes
Makes: 4 servings

- 2 **6-ounce skinless, boneless chicken breast halves**
- ¼ **teaspoon salt**
- ⅛ **teaspoon ground black pepper**
- 2 **teaspoons lime juice**
- 2 **teaspoons olive oil**
- 4 **slices thick-cut bacon**
- 1 **cup mayonnaise**
- 2 **anchovy fillets, finely chopped**
- 2 **tablespoons white wine vinegar**
- ⅓ **cup chopped fresh flat-leaf parsley**
- ¼ **cup chopped fresh chives**
- 2 **tablespoons water**
- 2 **teaspoons lime juice**
  Pinch of sugar
- 1 **head iceberg lettuce, chopped**
- 2 **hard-cooked eggs, peeled and finely chopped**
- 1 **ripe avocado, pitted, peeled, and diced**
- 1 **cup crumbled Roquefort cheese or blue cheese (4 ounces)**

1 Toss chicken with salt, pepper, and lime juice. Heat oil in a large nonstick skillet over medium-high heat for 1 minute. Add chicken; cover skillet and cook until golden brown, 6 to 7 minutes. Turn chicken, cover and cook for 6 to 7 minutes more, or until instant-read thermometer inserted in thickest portion of each breast registers 170°F. Wrap chicken in a large piece of foil and seal. Cool for 20 minutes, then dice.

2 Meanwhile, cook bacon in same skillet over medium heat until crisp, 7 to 8 minutes. Drain.

3 For dressing, combine mayonnaise, anchovies, vinegar, parsley, chives, water, lime juice, and sugar in bowl.

4 Arrange lettuce on a large platter, then arrange chicken, eggs, avocado, cheese, and bacon in rows over top. Serve with dressing.

Nutrition facts per serving: 840 cal., 73 g total fat (17 g sat. fat), 222 mg chol., 1228 mg sodium, 15 g carb., 4 g dietary fiber, 35 g protein.

tuscan CHICKEN-RICE SALAD

Prep: 30 minutes
Chill: 4 to 24 hours
Makes: 6 servings

2 **cups water**

1 **cup long grain rice**

1 **2.25-ounce can sliced black olives, drained**

½ **cup bottled roasted red sweet peppers, drained and chopped**

½ **cup cooked or canned chickpeas (garbanzo beans), drained**

¼ **cup thinly sliced scallions (2)**

1 **6- or 6.5-ounce jar marinated artichoke hearts**

12 **ounces skinless, boneless chicken breast halves, cut into bite-size strips**

2 **teaspoons chili powder**

½ **teaspoon dried rosemary, crushed**

½ **cup crumbled feta cheese with basil and tomato or crumbled plain feta (2 ounces)**

1 In a medium saucepan, combine water and rice. Bring to boiling; reduce heat. Simmer, covered, for about 15 minutes or until water is absorbed. Place rice in colander; rinse with cold water. Set aside to drain.

2 In a large bowl, combine olives, roasted peppers, chickpeas, and scallions. Drain artichokes, reserving marinade. Chop artichokes; add to olive mixture. Stir in cooked rice.

3 Sprinkle chicken with chili powder and rosemary. In a large nonstick skillet, heat 1 tablespoon of the reserved artichoke marinade over medium heat; add chicken. Cook for 3 to 4 minutes or until no longer pink. Add chicken and remaining artichoke marinade to rice mixture. Add feta cheese; toss gently to combine. Cover and chill for 4 to 24 hours.

Nutrition facts per serving: 261 cal., 6 g total fat (2 g sat. fat), 41 mg chol., 401 mg sodium, 33 g carb., 2 g dietary fiber, 18 g protein.

sesame AND GINGER CHICKEN SALAD

Start to Finish: 20 minutes
Makes: 4 servings

- 1 **pound skinless, boneless chicken breast, cut into bite-size strips**
- **Salt and ground black pepper**
- ¼ **cup bottled light Asian-style dressing with sesame and ginger**
- 2 **cups packaged julienned carrots**
- ⅛ **teaspoon crushed red pepper**
- 1 **head butterhead lettuce, leaves separated**
- ¼ **cup honey-roasted peanuts, chopped**
- **Lime wedges**

1 Sprinkle chicken lightly with salt and black pepper. Lightly coat a large skillet with cooking spray; heat over medium-high heat. Add chicken; cook and stir for 3 minutes or until browned. Add 1 tablespoon of the dressing and the carrots to skillet; cook and stir for 2 to 3 minutes more or until carrots are crisp-tender and chicken is no longer pink. Stir in red pepper.

2 Stack lettuce on plates. Top with chicken-carrot mixture. Sprinkle with chopped nuts. Serve with remaining dressing and lime wedges.

Nutrition facts per serving: 231 cal., 7 g total fat (1 g sat. fat), 66 mg chol., 436 mg sodium, 12 g carb., 3 g dietary fiber, 29 g protein.

citrus-chicken SALAD

This garden-fresh spinach salad is a terrific way to use up leftover chicken. Or when you're cooking chicken breasts, add an extra piece or two so there's some left over.

Prep: 20 minutes
Chill: Overnight
Makes: 2 servings

6 ounces cooked chicken breast, shredded, or one 6-ounce package refrigerated cooked chicken breast strips*

2 cups fresh baby spinach

1 11-ounce can mandarin orange sections, drained

½ cup loose-pack frozen whole kernel corn

2 tablespoons white wine vinegar or cider vinegar

1 tablespoon Dijon-style mustard

2 teaspoons snipped fresh oregano, or ½ teaspoon dried oregano, crushed

2 teaspoons low-sugar or low-calorie orange marmalade

2 teaspoons salad oil

⅛ teaspoon salt

⅛ teaspoon ground black pepper

1 Divide chicken between two small resealable freezer bags.

2 Divide spinach, mandarin oranges, and corn between two airtight storage containers. In a screw-top jar, combine vinegar, mustard, oregano, orange marmalade, oil, salt, and pepper; cover and shake well. Divide dressing mixture between two small resealable plastic bags. Chill salads and dressing overnight. Freeze chicken overnight.

3 Just before serving, add the dressing and chicken to the spinach mixture. Toss to coat.

Nutrition facts per serving: 304 cal., 8 g total fat (2 g sat. fat), 72 mg chol., 422 mg sodium, 28 g carb., 3 g dietary fiber, 31 g protein.

*Tip: If using the packaged refrigerated cooked chicken breast strips, omit the ⅛ teaspoon salt from the dressing.

cool-as-a-cucumber
CHICKEN SALAD

Start to Finish: 25 minutes
Makes: 4 to 6 servings

2 **cups shredded cooked chicken (10 ounces)**

2 **cups purchased cut-up cantaloupe or halved seedless red grapes**

1 **cup chopped cucumber**

⅓ **cup orange juice**

3 **tablespoons salad oil**

1 **tablespoon snipped fresh mint or cilantro**

  Salt and ground black pepper

4 **cups shredded romaine or leaf lettuce**

1 In a large bowl, toss together chicken, cantaloupe, and cucumber.

2 For dressing, in a screw-top jar combine orange juice, oil, and mint. Cover and shake well. Season to taste with salt and pepper. Drizzle dressing over chicken mixture; toss lightly to coat.

3 Arrange romaine on salad plates. Top with chicken mixture.

Nutrition facts per serving: 269 cal., 16 g total fat (3 g sat. fat), 62 mg chol., 114 mg sodium, 11 g carb., 1 g dietary fiber, 22 g protein.

chicken AND QUINOA SALAD WITH ROASTED CHILES

Prep: 45 minutes
Roast: 20 minutes
Stand: 45 minutes
Cook: 25 minutes
Oven: 425°F
Makes: 4 or 5 servings

8 ounces fresh Anaheim chile peppers, poblano chile peppers, banana chile peppers, and/or red sweet peppers*

1 cup quinoa**

1 cup water

3 tablespoons lime juice

2 tablespoons olive oil

2 cloves garlic, minced

¼ teaspoon salt

¼ teaspoon ground black pepper

1½ cups shredded cooked chicken

⅓ cup pine nuts or slivered almonds, toasted

½ cup coarsely chopped fresh cilantro

½ cup chopped scallions (4)

Bibb or Boston lettuce

1 Preheat oven to 425°F. Halve chile peppers lengthwise. Remove stems, seeds, and membranes. Place pepper halves, cut side down, on a foil-lined baking sheet. Roast for 20 to 25 minutes or until skins are blistered and dark. Carefully fold foil up and around pepper halves to enclose; let stand about 15 minutes. Using a sharp knife, loosen edges of the skins; gently and slowly pull off the skin in strips. Cut peppers into bite-size strips; set aside.

2 Place uncooked quinoa in a fine-mesh sieve; thoroughly rinse with cold water and drain. In a medium saucepan, combine quinoa and the 1 cup water. Bring to boiling; reduce heat. Simmer, covered, for 25 minutes. Remove from heat. Uncover; let stand about 30 minutes.

3 For dressing, in a small screw-top jar combine lime juice, olive oil, garlic, salt, and black pepper. Cover and shake well.

4 In a large bowl, combine cooked quinoa, roasted pepper strips, dressing, chicken, pine nuts, cilantro, and scallions; toss to combine. Line dinner plates with lettuce. Top with chicken salad.

Nutrition facts per serving: 454 cal., 22 g total fat (3 g sat. fat), 50 mg chol., 220 mg sodium, 43 g carb., 5 g dietary fiber, 26 g protein.

***Tip:** Because hot chile peppers contain volatile oils that can burn your skin and eyes, avoid direct contact with peppers as much as possible. When working with chile peppers, wear plastic or rubber gloves. If your bare hands do touch the peppers, wash your hands well with soap and water.

****Tip:** If desired, substitute 2 cups couscous for the quinoa.

chicken AND SPINACH SALAD WITH AVOCADO DRESSING

Start to Finish: 40 minutes
Makes: 8 servings

- 1 **6-ounce package fresh baby spinach (about 6 cups)**
- 4 **cups chopped or shredded cooked chicken**
- 1 **medium cucumber, halved lengthwise, seeded, and sliced**
- 1 **cup cherry tomatoes, halved**
- 2 **medium red, yellow, and/or green sweet peppers, cut into thin strips**
- 1 **small red onion, thinly sliced**
- ¼ **cup snipped fresh cilantro**
- 1 **large ripe avocado, pitted, peeled, and cut up**
- 2 **cloves garlic, minced**
- 2 **tablespoons lime juice**
- 2 **teaspoons finely shredded lime zest**
- ⅔ **cup light sour cream**
- 2 **tablespoons snipped fresh cilantro**
- ½ **teaspoon salt**
- ⅛ **teaspoon ground black pepper**
-   **Bottled hot pepper sauce**

1 In a large serving bowl, toss together spinach, chicken, cucumber, cherry tomatoes, sweet peppers, half of the sliced red onion, and cilantro. Set aside.

2 For dressing, in a food processor* combine avocado, remaining red onion, garlic, and lime juice. Cover and process until mixture is smooth. Stir in lime zest, sour cream, cilantro, salt, and pepper. Season to taste with bottled hot pepper sauce. If desired, stir in 1 to 2 tablespoons water to make dressing of desired consistency.

3 Spoon dressing over spinach mixture. Toss gently to combine.

Nutrition facts per serving: 214 cal., 10 g total fat (3 g sat. fat), 68 mg chol., 241 mg sodium, 9 g carb., 3 g dietary fiber, 23 g protein.

*Tip: If you don't have a food processor, mash avocado with a fork or a potato masher. Finely chop the onion. Stir ingredients together.

warm POLENTA-ZUCCHINI SALAD WITH CHICKEN

Save time by cooking the chicken a day ahead; then simply heat it up in the skillet when you're ready to serve.

Start to Finish: 25 minutes
Prep: 15 minutes
Makes: 4 servings

2 **medium zucchini**

Salt and ground black pepper

3½ **tablespoons extra-virgin olive oil**

½ **16-ounce package prepared polenta, cut into ¾-inch cubes**

2 **tablespoons red wine vinegar**

1 **tablespoon chopped oregano**

½ **teaspoon sugar**

½ **teaspoon kosher salt**

5 **cups baby mixed greens or baby arugula**

2 **skinless, boneless chicken breasts, cooked and shredded (1¾ cups total)**

½ **cup crumbled blue cheese (3 ounces)**

1 Cut zucchini in half lengthwise, then on the bias into ¼-inch slices, and sprinkle with salt and pepper. Heat ½ tablespoon oil in a large nonstick skillet over high heat and add zucchini. Cook, stirring, until just golden, about 2 minutes. Remove zucchini, then reduce heat to medium and add polenta to skillet. Cook, stirring, until just heated through, about 4 minutes.

2 Whisk together vinegar, oregano, sugar, salt, and remaining 3 tablespoons olive oil. In a large bowl, toss half the vinaigrette with the greens, chicken, zucchini, and polenta. Arrange on a platter and sprinkle with blue cheese. Serve with remaining vinaigrette.

Nutrition facts per serving: 350 cal., 20.5 g total fat (6.5 g sat. fat), 69 mg chol., 583 mg sodium, 10 g carb., 2 g dietary fiber, 27 g protein.

chicken SALAD WITH PEANUT DRESSING

Dress up leftover cooked chicken with this fabulous peanut butter, soy sauce, and ginger dressing.

Start to Finish: 30 minutes
Makes: 4 servings

- 6 **cups coarsely torn napa cabbage or romaine lettuce**
- 2 **cups coarsely shredded cooked chicken breast (about 10 ounces)**
- 1 **small apple, cored and coarsely chopped**
- ½ **cup seedless red and/or green grapes, halved**
- 3 **tablespoons water**
- 2 **tablespoons creamy peanut butter**
- 2 **teaspoons reduced-sodium soy sauce**
- ¼ **teaspoon ground ginger**

Divide cabbage among serving plates. Top with chicken, apple, and grapes. In a small bowl, whisk together the water, peanut butter, soy sauce, and ground ginger. Drizzle over salads.

Nutrition facts per serving: 209 cal., 7 g total fat (2 g sat. fat), 60 mg chol., 188 mg sodium, 12 g carb., 3 g dietary fiber, 26 g protein.

spring GREENS AND ROASTED CHICKEN SALAD

1 2¼-pound purchased roasted chicken, chilled

1 5-ounce package mixed spring greens salad mix (about 8 cups)

2 cups fresh sliced strawberries or blueberries

4 ounces Gorgonzola or blue cheese, crumbled (1 cup)

½ cup honey-roasted cashews or peanuts

1 lemon, halved

3 tablespoons olive oil

¼ teaspoon salt

¼ teaspoon ground black pepper

1 Remove string from chicken, if present. Remove and discard skin from chicken. Pull meat from bones, discarding bones. Shred meat (you should have about 3½ cups).

2 Place greens on a platter. Top with chicken, berries, cheese, and nuts. Drizzle with juice from lemon and oil; sprinkle with salt and pepper.

Nutrition facts per serving: 426 cal., 31 g total fat (9 g sat. fat), 81 mg chol., 482 mg sodium, 12 g carb., 2 g dietary fiber, 28 g protein.

chicken-mango SALAD

Our quick-to-fix supper salad uses convenience food products to make it easy for the cook. It's full of flavor from the variety of fruit and the dressing.

Start to Finish: 25 minutes
Makes: 4 servings

⅓ **cup dried cherries, cranberries, blueberries, or currants**

1 **2- to 2½-pound purchased roasted chicken**

½ **cup bottled balsamic vinaigrette salad dressing**

2 **tablespoons orange juice**

1 **10-ounce package torn romaine lettuce or torn mixed greens (8 cups)**

½ **of an 8-ounce package presliced mushrooms**

1½ **cups fresh or refrigerated grapefruit sections, mango slices, and/or papaya slices, drained**

2 **tablespoons dry-roasted shelled sunflower seeds**

1 In a small bowl, pour enough boiling water over cherries to cover. Let stand for 5 minutes; drain. Meanwhile, use two forks to pull chicken meat off the bones and shred in large pieces. Discard bones and skin. Measure 2 cups chicken pieces and place in a medium bowl; set aside. Cover and chill remaining chicken for another use.

2 For dressing, in a screw-top jar combine the balsamic vinaigrette and orange juice. Cover and shake well.

3 To serve, arrange lettuce on dinner plates or on a platter. Top each with mushrooms and grapefruit sections. Arrange chicken in center of each salad. Sprinkle salads with cherries and sunflower seeds. Drizzle the dressing evenly over the salads.

Nutrition facts per serving: 325 cal., 17 g total fat (3 g sat. fat), 62 mg chol., 422 mg sodium, 22 g carb., 3 g dietary fiber, 24 g protein.

soups

Chicken Tortilla Soup, *page 93*

cheesy CHICKEN CHOWDER

Prep: 25 minutes
Cook: 15 minutes
Makes: 16 servings

1 large onion, chopped
    (1 cup)

1 cup thinly sliced celery

2 cloves garlic, minced

1 tablespoon cooking oil

1½ pounds skinless, boneless
    chicken breast halves,
    cut into bite-size pieces

2 14-ounce cans chicken
    broth

1 32-ounce package frozen
    diced hash-brown
    potatoes

1 2.64-ounce envelopes
    country gravy mix

2 cups milk

1 8-ounce package process
    cheese spread, cut into
    chunks

1 16-ounce jar chunky salsa

1 4.5-ounce can diced green
    chile peppers

Corn chips

1 In a 6-quart Dutch oven, cook and stir onion, celery, and garlic in hot oil over medium heat about for 5 minutes or until onion is tender. Add chicken; cook and stir for about 3 minutes or until no longer pink. Add broth and potatoes. Bring to boiling; reduce heat. Simmer, covered, for 12 to 15 minutes or until potatoes are tender, stirring occasionally.

2 Meanwhile, in a medium bowl, dissolve gravy mix in milk. Stir milk mixture into soup mixture. Stir in cheese, salsa and green chiles; reduce heat to low. Cook and stir until cheese is melted. Serve with corn chips.

Nutrition facts per serving: 303 cal., 15 g total fat (5 g sat. fat), 35 mg chol., 857 mg sodium, 26 g carb., 2 g dietary fiber, 16 g protein.

chicken AND WILD RICE SOUP

Prep: 30 minutes
Cook: 50 minutes
Makes: 4 servings

½ **cup finely chopped carrot (1 medium)**

½ **cup finely chopped onion (1 medium)**

½ **cup finely chopped celery (1 stalk)**

1 **tablespoon butter or margarine**

4 **cups chicken broth**

¾ **cup wild rice, rinsed and drained**

12 **ounces skinless, boneless chicken breast halves, cut into ¾-inch pieces**

2 **tablespoons all-purpose flour**

2 **tablespoons butter or margarine, softened**

2 **cups half-and-half or light cream**

Salt and ground black pepper

① In a large Dutch oven, cook and stir carrot, onion, and celery in hot butter for 5 minutes or until tender. Add broth and wild rice. Bring to boiling; reduce heat. Simmer, covered, for 30 minutes. Add chicken pieces. Simmer, covered, for 20 to 25 minutes more or until wild rice is tender.

② In a small bowl, combine flour and softened butter to make a smooth paste. Stir flour mixture into the rice mixture. Cook and stir until thickened and bubbly. Cook and stir for 1 minute more. Add half-and-half. Cook and stir over medium heat until heated through. Season to taste with salt and pepper.

Nutrition facts per serving: 479 cal., 24 g total fat (14 g sat. fat), 119 mg chol., 1213 mg sodium, 36 g carb., 3 g dietary fiber, 30 g protein.

chicken AND KALE SOUP

Start to Finish: 40 minutes
Makes: 6 servings

⅓ **cup finely chopped onion**

2 **cloves garlic, minced**

1 **tablespoon extra-virgin olive oil**

1 **pound skinless, boneless chicken breast halves, cut into 1-inch pieces, or 1 pound ground turkey breast**

4 **cups reduced-sodium chicken broth**

1 **15-ounce can garbanzo beans (chickpeas), rinsed and drained**

1 **14.5-ounce can no-salt-added diced tomatoes, undrained**

1 **tablespoon dried Italian seasoning, crushed**

½ **teaspoon sea salt or salt**

½ **teaspoon coarsely ground black pepper**

1 **cup dried whole wheat or whole grain penne**

2 **cups chopped kale or spinach**

1 In a 4-quart Dutch oven, cook and stir onion and garlic in hot oil over medium-high heat for 3 to 4 minutes or until onion is tender. Add chicken. Cook and stir for 4 to 5 minutes more or until chicken is no longer pink.

2 Stir chicken broth, garbanzo beans, tomatoes, Italian seasoning, salt, and pepper into Dutch oven. Bring to boiling; stir in pasta. Return to boiling; reduce heat to medium. Cook, covered, for about 12 minutes or until pasta is tender, stirring occasionally. Remove Dutch oven from heat; stir in kale. Cover and let stand for 2 minutes before serving.

Nutrition facts per serving: 249 cal., 5 g total fat (1 g sat. fat), 44 mg chol., 842 mg sodium, 25 g carb., 4 g dietary fiber, 25 g protein.

chicken-squash NOODLE SOUP

Start to Finish: 40 minutes
Makes: 6 servings

1 **pound skinless, boneless chicken breast halves, cut into 1-inch pieces**

½ **teaspoon poultry seasoning**

1 **tablespoon canola oil**

1 **medium onion, chopped**

1 **stalk celery, chopped**

1 **medium carrot, peeled and chopped**

2 **cloves garlic, minced**

3 **14-ounce cans reduced-sodium chicken broth**

1½ **cups dried medium noodles**

1 **medium zucchini or yellow summer squash, quartered lengthwise and cut into 1-inch-thick pieces**

1¾ **cups fat-free milk**

¼ **cup all-purpose flour**

¼ **cup snipped fresh parsley**

1 In a large bowl, combine chicken pieces and poultry seasoning; toss to coat. In a 4-quart Dutch oven, heat oil over medium heat. Add chicken pieces; cook for 3 to 5 minutes or until chicken pieces are browned. Using a slotted spoon, transfer chicken to a bowl.

2 In the same Dutch oven, cook onion, celery, carrot, and garlic over medium heat about 5 minutes or just until tender, stirring occasionally. Add chicken broth; bring to boiling. Add chicken, noodles, and zucchini. Return to boiling; reduce heat. Cover and simmer for 5 minutes.

3 In a medium bowl, whisk milk and flour together until combined; stir into chicken mixture. Cook and stir until bubbly. Cook and stir for 1 minute more. Sprinkle with parsley just before serving.

Nutrition facts per serving: 215 cal., 4 g total fat (1 g sat. fat), 53 mg chol., 560 mg sodium, 20 g carb., 2 g dietary fiber, 25 g protein.

chicken AND VEGETABLE SOUP

The barley adds texture and flavor to this colorful soup.

Prep: 45 minutes
Cook: 15 minutes
Makes: 8 servings

2 **pounds skinless, boneless chicken breast halves, cut into bite-size pieces**

1 **teaspoon poultry seasoning**

2 **tablespoons olive oil**

1½ **cups chopped fresh mushrooms**

1 **cup chopped carrot**

½ **cup chopped onion**

½ **cup chopped green sweet pepper**

4 **cloves garlic, minced**

2 **tablespoons snipped fresh basil, or 2 teaspoons dried basil, crushed**

1 **tablespoon snipped fresh parsley, or 1 teaspoon dried parsley, crushed**

¼ **teaspoon ground black pepper**

⅛ **teaspoon salt**

6 **cups water**

2 **tablespoons chicken bouillon granules**

1 **pound potatoes, cut into 1-inch pieces (about 2¾ cups)**

½ **cup quick-cooking barley**

1 In a medium bowl, toss chicken breast pieces with the poultry seasoning; set aside.

2 In a 5- to 6-quart Dutch oven, heat 1 tablespoon of the oil over medium heat. Add mushrooms, carrot, onion, sweet pepper, garlic, dried basil and parsley (if using), black pepper, and salt; cook for 10 minutes, stirring occasionally. Remove vegetables from Dutch oven.

3 Add the remaining 1 tablespoon oil to the Dutch oven; heat over medium heat. Add chicken pieces; cook about 5 minutes or until browned, stirring occasionally. Return vegetables to Dutch oven. Stir in the water and chicken bouillon granules. Bring to boiling; stir in potatoes and barley. Return to boiling; reduce heat. Cover and simmer for about 15 minutes or until potatoes are tender. Stir in fresh basil and parsley (if using).

Nutrition facts per serving: 249 cal., 5 g total fat (1 g sat. fat), 66 mg chol., 705 mg sodium, 20 g carb., 3 g dietary fiber, 29 g protein.

cream OF CHICKEN AND CHEESE SOUP

Although this recipe includes a can of condensed soup, tender chicken and sharp American cheese give it a delightful homemade flavor.

Start to Finish: 40 minutes
Makes: 4 servings

- 2 **cups water**
- 1 **small whole chicken breast (about 12 ounces)**
- 1 **small onion, chopped (⅓ cup)**
- 1 **small carrot, chopped (⅓ cup)**
- 1 **small stalk celery, chopped (⅓ cup)**
- 1 **10.75-ounce can condensed cream of chicken soup**
- ½ **cup milk**
- 2 **ounces American cheese, cubed (about ½ cup)**

Shredded American cheese (optional)

1 In a large saucepan, bring the water to boiling. Add chicken breast. Return to boiling; reduce heat. Cover and simmer for 20 to 25 minutes or until chicken is tender and no longer pink. Remove chicken.

2 Add onion, carrot, and celery to cooking liquid. Return to boiling; reduce heat. Simmer, uncovered, for 10 minutes.

3 When cool enough to handle, remove chicken from bones; discard bones. Chop the chicken. Stir soup and milk into vegetable mixture until smooth. Add chicken and cubed cheese; heat and stir until cheese melts. If desired, garnish with shredded cheese.

Nutrition facts per serving: 209 cal., 11 g total fat (5 g sat. fat), 47 mg chol., 820 mg sodium, 11 g carb., 1 g dietary fiber, 16 g protein.

tortellini CHICKEN SOUP

Just a pinch of saffron goes a long way in adding flavor and more intense color to food. The aromatic spice is a tad expensive, so feel free to leave it out. This soup is terrific with or without it.

Start to Finish: 25 minutes
Makes: 4 servings

12 ounces skinless, boneless chicken breast halves, cut into ½-inch cubes

6 cups reduced-sodium chicken broth

½ cup sliced leek or chopped onion

1 tablespoon grated fresh ginger

¼ teaspoon saffron threads, slightly crushed (optional)

1 9-ounce package refrigerated herb-chicken tortellini or vegetable ravioli

½ cup baby spinach leaves or shredded spinach

1 Lightly coat a large saucepan with nonstick cooking spray. Preheat over medium-high heat. Add chicken; cook and stir for 3 minutes. Carefully add broth, leek or onion, ginger, and (if desired) saffron.

2 Bring to boiling. Add tortellini or ravioli. Return to boiling; reduce heat. Simmer, uncovered, for 5 to 9 minutes or until tortellini or ravioli is tender, stirring occasionally. Remove from heat. Top individual servings with spinach.

Nutrition facts per serving: 222 cal., 3 g total fat (0 g sat. fat), 59 mg chol., 1221 mg sodium, 21 g carb., 3 g dietary fiber, 29 g protein.

thai CHICKEN SOUP

Prep: 25 minutes
Cook: 20 minutes
Makes: 6 servings

2   tablespoons grated
    fresh ginger
3   cloves garlic, minced
1   tablespoon olive oil
1   cup chopped onions
    (2 medium)
4   cups chicken broth
1   pound skinless, boneless
    chicken breast halves,
    cut into ¾-inch pieces
2   cups bias-sliced carrots
    (4 medium)
1   teaspoon finely shredded
    lemon zest
¼   teaspoon crushed red
    pepper
1   14-ounce can unsweetened
    coconut milk
1   medium red sweet
    pepper, cut into ½-inch
    pieces
2   4-ounce cans sliced
    mushrooms, drained
¼   cup snipped fresh cilantro
⅓   cup chopped roasted
    peanuts
    Lime wedges (optional)

1 In a 4-quart Dutch oven, cook and stir ginger and garlic in hot oil over medium heat for 30 seconds. Add onions; cook and stir for 4 to 6 minutes or until onion is tender but not brown. Stir in the broth; bring to boiling. Add chicken, carrots, lemon zest, and crushed red pepper. Return to boiling; reduce heat. Cover and simmer for 15 to 20 minutes or until chicken and carrots are tender.

2 Stir coconut milk, sweet pepper, and mushrooms into soup; heat through. Top each serving with cilantro and peanuts. If desired, serve with lime wedges to squeeze over soup.

Nutrition facts per serving: 413 cal., 26 g total fat (15 g sat. fat), 67 mg chol., 844 mg sodium, 15 g carb., 3 g dietary fiber, 30 g protein.

quick ASIAN CHICKEN SOUP

Canned soup instantly turns into a zesty Asian soup with the help of frozen Asian veggies, ginger, and soy sauce.

Start to Finish: 15 minutes
Makes: 4 servings

2½ **cups water**

2 **10.5-ounce cans condensed chicken with rice soup**

2 **cups loose-pack frozen broccoli stir-fry vegetables (broccoli, carrots, onions, red peppers, celery, water chestnuts, and mushrooms)**

1 **tablespoon soy sauce**

½ **teaspoon ground ginger**

2 **cups chopped cooked chicken or turkey (about 10 ounces)**

1 In a large saucepan, combine the water and the soup. Bring to boiling.

2 Stir in frozen vegetables, soy sauce, and ginger. Return to boiling; reduce heat. Simmer, covered, for 3 to 5 minutes or until vegetables are tender.

3 Stir in chicken; heat through.

Nutrition facts per serving: 247 cal., 9 g total fat (3 g sat. fat), 72 mg chol., 1479 mg sodium, 14 g carb., 1 g dietary fiber, 27 g protein.

chicken TORTILLA SOUP

Serve the tortilla chips on the side or break up a few in the bottom of the bowls and ladle the soup over them.

Start to Finish: 25 minutes
Makes: 4 servings

2 **14-ounce cans chicken broth with roasted garlic**

1 **14.5-ounce can Mexican-style stewed tomatoes, undrained**

2 **cups chopped cooked chicken**

2 **cups frozen sweet pepper and onion stir-fry vegetables**

Tortilla chips

Sliced fresh jalapeño chile peppers (optional)

Lime wedges (optional)

1 In a large saucepan, combine chicken broth, tomatoes, chicken, and frozen vegetables. Bring to boiling; reduce heat. Cover and simmer for 5 minutes.

2 To serve, ladle soup into warm soup bowls. Serve with tortilla chips. If desired, top with sliced jalapeño chile peppers and serve with lime wedges.

Nutrition facts per serving: 266 cal., 9 g total fat (2 g sat. fat), 65 mg chol., 1260 mg sodium, 22 g carb., 1 g dietary fiber, 24 g protein.

mulligatawny SOUP

The unusual name of this soup reflects its origin in southern India. In Victorian times, English visitors enjoyed it there and introduced the recipe to cooks at home.

Prep: 25 minutes
Cook: 30 minutes
Makes: 8 servings

- 2 **medium carrots, chopped**
- 2 **large onions, chopped**
- 2 **medium potatoes, chopped**
- 1 **teaspoon bottled minced garlic (2 cloves)**
- 2 **tablespoons butter or margarine**
- 3 **14-ounce cans chicken broth**
- 1 **15-ounce can chickpeas (garbanzo beans), rinsed and drained**
- 1 **cup diced cooked chicken (about 5 ounces)**
- 1 **cup unsweetened coconut milk**
- 4 **teaspoons curry powder**
- 1 **apple, cored and chopped**
- ¼ **cup snipped fresh cilantro**

In a 4-quart Dutch oven, cook carrots, onions, potatoes, and garlic in hot butter over medium heat for about 10 minutes or until the onion is tender. Add chicken broth; cook over medium-low heat for about 20 minutes or until the vegetables are tender. Stir in chickpeas, chicken, coconut milk, and curry powder; heat through. Top individual servings with apple and cilantro.

Nutrition facts per serving: 267 cal., 14 g total fat (9 g sat. fat), 24 mg chol., 878 mg sodium, 26 g carb., 6 g dietary fiber, 12 g protein.

chicken NOODLE SOUP

Prep: 20 minutes
Cook: 15 minutes
Makes: 4 servings

4½ cups chicken broth

1 cup chopped onion
(1 large)

1 cup sliced carrots
(2 medium)

1 cup sliced celery (2 stalks)

1 teaspoon dried basil,
crushed

1 teaspoon dried oregano,
crushed

¼ teaspoon ground black
pepper

1 bay leaf

1½ cups dried medium
noodles

2 cups cubed cooked
chicken or turkey
(12 ounces)

In a large saucepan, combine broth, onion, carrots, celery, basil, oregano, pepper, and bay leaf. Bring to boiling; reduce heat. Simmer, covered, for 5 minutes. Stir in noodles. Return to boiling; reduce heat. Cover and simmer for 8 to 10 minutes or until noodles are tender but still firm and vegetables are just tender. Discard bay leaf. Stir in chicken; heat through.

Nutrition facts per serving: 241 cal., 7 g total fat (2 g sat. fat), 77 mg chol., 1190 mg sodium, 20 g carb., 3 g dietary fiber, 24 g protein.

Chicken Tortellini Soup: Prepare as above, except substitute small broccoli florets for the celery and one 9-ounce package refrigerated cheese-filled tortellini for the noodles. Add the broccoli and 1 cup sliced fresh mushrooms with the pasta.

Parmesan-Pesto Chicken Noodle Soup: Prepare as above, except substitute 1 small zucchini, halved lengthwise and sliced, for the celery and Italian seasoning for the basil and oregano. Add 2 cloves garlic, minced, to the broth mixture. Substitute dried small shell macaroni for the egg noodles; add zucchini with the pasta. Meanwhile, spread 4 slices of Italian bread with 1 tablespoon basil pesto each. Sprinkle each with 1 tablespoon finely shredded Parmesan cheese. Place, spread side up, on a baking sheet. Broil 3 to 4 inches from the heat for about 2 minutes or until cheese melts. Top each serving of soup with a slice of the bread.

simply RAMEN CHICKEN SOUP

Start to Finish: 15 minutes
Makes: 4 servings

2 **14-ounce cans reduced-sodium chicken broth**

2 **3-ounce packages chicken-flavored ramen noodles**

½ **teaspoon dried oregano or basil, crushed**

1 **10-ounce package frozen cut broccoli**

2 **cups shredded or cubed cooked chicken or turkey**

¼ **cup toasted sliced almonds**

In a large saucepan, bring chicken broth, the seasonings from the flavoring packet from noodles, and oregano or basil to boiling. Break up noodles. Add noodles and broccoli to mixture in saucepan; return to boiling. Reduce heat; simmer, uncovered, for 3 minutes. Stir in chicken; heat through. Ladle soup into bowls. Sprinkle with almonds.

Nutrition facts per serving: 403 cal., 18 g total fat (2 g sat. fat), 62 mg chol., 1329 mg sodium, 32 g carb., 3 g dietary fiber, 32 g protein.

chicken MATZO BALL SOUP

Prep: 45 minutes
Cook: 2 hours
Makes: 12 side-dish
servings

- 1 4- to 5-pound roasting chicken
- 2½ quarts water
- 1½ cups sliced celery (3 stalks)
- 1 cup chopped onions (2 medium)
- ½ cup sliced leek (1 large)
- 1 tablespoon salt
- ¼ teaspoon ground black pepper
- 1 cup sliced carrots (2 medium)
- 1 cup sliced parsnips (2 medium)
- 4 or 5 fresh parsley sprigs
- 4 sprigs fresh dill, or ¼ teaspoon dried dill (optional)
- Matzo Balls*

1 Place chicken in an 8- to 10-quart stockpot. Add the water, celery, onions, leek, salt, and pepper. Bring to boiling; reduce heat. Cover and simmer for 1½ hours. Add carrots and parsnips; cover and simmer for about 30 minutes more or until vegetables are tender and chicken is no longer pink (180°F in thighs).

2 Remove chicken from pot. When cool enough to handle, remove and discard skin from chicken. Pull meat from bones, discarding bones. (Cover and chill meat for another use.)

3 Using a slotted spoon, remove vegetables from broth. Strain broth through two layers of 100% cotton cheesecloth placed in a colander; discard solids. Skim fat from broth. Return broth and vegetables to pot. Add parsley and, if desired, dill; heat through. Serve in bowls with Matzo Balls.

*Matzo Balls: In a large mixing bowl, combine 1 cup matzo meal, 1 teaspoon salt, and pinch of ground black pepper. Beat in 4 lightly beaten eggs and ¼ cup chicken fat (schmaltz) until well blended. Stir in ¼ cup carbonated water. Cover and chill for at least 2 hours. With wet hands, shape dough into 1-inch balls. Carefully drop dough into a large pot of gently boiling salted water. Cover and simmer for 30 minutes or until matzo balls are light and cooked all the way through. Do not uncover pot until end of cooking. Using a slotted spoon, carefully remove matzo balls. Serve in hot soup. Makes about 30.

Nutrition facts per serving: 276 cal., 14 g total fat (4 g sat. fat), 127 mg chol., 451 mg sodium, 16 g carb., 2 g dietary fiber, 20 g protein.

chicken POSOLE SOUP WITH TORTILLAS

Prep: 30 minutes
Cook: 30 minutes
Makes: 8 servings

1   2- to 2½-pound deli-
    roasted chicken

¾   cup chopped yellow
    onion (1 large)

2   teaspoons ground cumin

1   teaspoon chili powder

2   teaspoons cooking oil

2   14-ounce cans reduced-
    sodium chicken broth

1   28-ounce can peeled roma
    tomatoes in puree,
    undrained, cut up*

1   15-ounce can yellow or
    white hominy, drained

1   10-ounce package frozen
    whole kernel corn

2   4-ounce cans diced green
    chile peppers

1   cup shredded Mexican
    cheese blend (4 ounces)

    Snipped fresh cilantro,
    halved grape tomatoes,
    chopped avocado,
    and/or corn tortilla chips

    Lime wedges (optional)

1 Remove and discard skin from chicken. Pull meat from bones, discarding bones. Cube meat (you should have about 3½ cups).

2 In a 4-quart Dutch oven, cook onion, cumin, and chili powder in hot oil over medium heat for 4 to 6 minutes or until onion is tender. Add chicken, broth, roma tomatoes, hominy, corn, and chile peppers. Bring to boiling; reduce heat. Simmer, uncovered, for 30 minutes, stirring occasionally.

3 To serve, ladle into bowls. Top with cheese, cilantro, grape tomatoes, avocado, and/or tortilla chips. If desired, serve with lime wedges to squeeze over soup.

Nutrition facts per serving: 392 cal., 21 g total fat (7 g sat. fat), 75 mg chol., 1191 mg sodium, 32 g carb., 7 g dietary fiber, 22 g protein.

*Tip: Use a pair of clean kitchen shears to cut up the tomatoes in the can.

chicken-butternut
SQUASH SOUP

If your family prefers small pieces of chicken, remove the meat from the bones, chop it in bite-size chunks, and stir into the soup.

Start to Finish: 45 minutes
Oven: 425°F/350°F
Makes: 6 servings

1¼ pounds butternut squash, peeled, seeded, and cut in ¾-inch pieces (4 cups)

1 small red onion, cut in ½-inch wedges

1 tablespoon curry powder

1 tablespoon olive oil

3 14-ounce cans reduced-sodium chicken broth

1 15- to 16-ounce can garbanzo beans (chickpeas), rinsed and drained

⅓ cup dried apricots, snipped

½ cup chopped walnuts

1 teaspoon olive oil

¼ teaspoon freshly grated or ground nutmeg

1 deli-roasted chicken, cut up

Fresh cilantro leaves

1 Preheat oven to 425°F. In a shallow roasting pan, toss squash and onion with curry powder and the 1 tablespoon oil. Roast, uncovered, for 20 minutes or until tender. Reduce oven temperature to 350°F.

2 In a 4-quart Dutch oven, combine roasted vegetables, broth, beans, and apricots. Bring to boiling; reduce heat. Simmer, covered, for 10 minutes. Transfer half of the soup to a food processor or blender. Cover; process or blend until smooth. Return to Dutch oven; heat through.

3 Meanwhile, in a bowl, toss walnuts with 1 teaspoon oil and the nutmeg. Spread nuts on a baking sheet. Bake for 7 minutes or until golden and toasted. Reheat chicken according to package directions, if needed.

4 To serve, top soup with nuts, chicken, and cilantro.

Nutrition facts per serving: 577 cal., 35 g total fat (9 g sat. fat), 167 mg chol., 1905 mg sodium, 30 g carb., 6 g dietary fiber, 44 g protein.

caraway CHICKEN AND VEGETABLE STEW

Prep: 30 minutes
Cook: 12 minutes
Makes: 6 servings

1 pound skinless, boneless chicken thighs or breast halves, trimmed of fat and cut into 1½-inch pieces

2 teaspoons olive oil

2 14-ounce cans reduced-sodium chicken broth

8 ounces green beans, trimmed and cut into 2-inch pieces

2 medium carrots, bias-cut into ½-inch-thick slices

2 stalks celery, bias-cut into ½-inch-thick slices

2 cups sliced fresh shiitake,* cremini, oyster,* and/or button mushrooms

1 cup frozen pearl onions

1¼ teaspoons caraway seeds, crushed

¼ teaspoon ground black pepper

¼ cup cold water

2 tablespoons cornstarch

1 In a 4-quart Dutch oven, cook chicken in hot oil over medium-high heat for 3 to 5 minutes or until browned, stirring occasionally. Add broth, beans, carrots, celery, mushrooms, onions, caraway seeds, and pepper. Bring to boiling; reduce heat. Simmer, covered, for 10 minutes or until vegetables are tender and chicken is no longer pink.

2 In a small bowl, combine the water and cornstarch; whisk until smooth. Add to stew. Cook and stir until thickened and bubbly. Cook and stir for 2 minutes more.

Nutrition facts per serving: 163 cal., 5 g total fat (1 g sat. fat), 63 mg chol., 410 mg sodium, 12 g carb., 3 g dietary fiber, 19 g protein.

*Tip: Remove stems from shiitake and oyster mushrooms before slicing.

moroccan CHICKEN STEW

Start to Finish: 35 minutes
Makes: 6 servings

1 tablespoon all-purpose
 flour

1 teaspoon ground
 coriander

1 teaspoon ground cumin

1 teaspoon ground paprika

½ teaspoon salt

½ teaspoon ground
 cinnamon

1 pound skinless, boneless
 chicken thighs, cut into
 1-inch pieces

2 medium onions, cut into
 wedges

3 cloves garlic, minced

1 tablespoon olive oil

1 28-ounce can crushed
 tomatoes, undrained

1 15-ounce can garbanzo
 beans (chickpeas), rinsed
 and drained

1½ cups water

½ cup raisins

⅓ cup small pitted black
 olives

3 cups hot cooked couscous

¼ cup snipped fresh cilantro

1 In a shallow bowl, combine flour, coriander, cumin, paprika, salt, and cinnamon. Coat chicken with the flour mixture.

2 In a 4-quart Dutch oven, cook onions and garlic in hot oil over medium heat for 4 to 6 minutes or until tender. Remove from Dutch oven, reserving oil in pan. Add chicken to pan, half at a time. Cook quickly until lightly browned, stirring frequently. Return all chicken and the onion mixture to pan. Add tomatoes, garbanzo beans, the water, raisins, and olives. Bring to boiling; reduce heat. Cover and simmer for about 10 minutes or until chicken is tender, stirring occasionally. Serve over couscous. Sprinkle with cilantro.

Nutrition facts per serving: 394 cal., 7 g total fat (1 g sat. fat), 60 mg chol., 858 mg sodium, 57 g carb., 8 g dietary fiber, 24 g protein.

caribbean CHICKEN STEW

Coconut milk, a staple in Caribbean kitchens, gives this stew a rich, thick body.

Prep: 50 minutes
Cook: 40 minutes
Makes: 8 servings

- 2 **medium onions, cut into 1-inch pieces**
- 1 **tablespoon cooking oil**
- 1 **3- to 3½-pound broiler-fryer chicken, cut into 8 pieces and wing tips removed**
- 2 **14-ounce cans chicken broth**
- 2½ **pounds sweet potatoes, peeled and cut into 1-inch pieces**
- 1 **14.5-ounce can diced tomatoes, undrained**
- 1 **10-ounce package frozen whole kernel corn**
- ½ **to 1 teaspoon crushed red pepper**
- ½ **teaspoon salt**
- 2 **tablespoons grated fresh ginger, or 1 teaspoon ground ginger**
- 1 **cup unsweetened coconut milk**
- 4 **cups hot cooked rice**

1 In a 4- to 5-quart Dutch oven, cook onions in hot oil over medium heat for about 5 minutes or until tender, stirring occasionally. Add chicken pieces and broth. Bring to boiling; reduce heat. Cover and simmer for 30 minutes. Transfer chicken to a bowl.

2 Add sweet potatoes, tomatoes, corn, red pepper, and salt to broth in Dutch oven. Return to boiling; reduce heat. Cover and simmer for 10 to 15 minutes or until vegetables are tender. Meanwhile, remove chicken meat from bones; discard bones and skin. Chop or shred meat.

3 Skim off fat. Using a slotted spoon, remove 1½ cups of the vegetables; remove 1 cup of the broth. Let cool slightly. Transfer to a blender or food processor. Cover and blend or process until smooth. Return to Dutch oven. Add chopped chicken and ginger to stew; heat through. Stir in coconut milk. Serve over hot cooked rice.

Nutrition facts per serving: 587 cal., 26 g total fat (10 g sat. fat), 86 mg chol., 731 mg sodium, 60 g carb., 5 g dietary fiber, 28 g protein.

chipotle CHILI WITH BEANS

Start to Finish: 25 minutes
Makes: 4 servings

8 ounces extra-lean ground beef, ground chicken breast, or ground turkey breast

1 cup chopped onion

1½ teaspoons ground cumin

2 14.5-ounce cans stewed tomatoes, undrained, cut up

1 15-ounce can red beans, rinsed and drained

1½ cups coarsely chopped red and/or yellow sweet pepper

½ cup water

2 to 3 teaspoons chopped canned chipotle chile peppers in adobo sauce*

1 tablespoon snipped fresh oregano

¼ cup shredded reduced-fat cheddar cheese

Lime wedges (optional)

Baked tortilla chips (optional)

1 Lightly coat a large saucepan with nonstick cooking spray. Preheat over medium heat. Add ground beef and onion; cook until browned. If necessary, drain off fat. Stir cumin into beef mixture in skillet; cook and stir for 1 minute more. Add tomatoes, red beans, sweet pepper, the water, and chile peppers. Bring to boiling; reduce heat. Cover and simmer for 5 minutes. Stir in oregano.

2 Spoon chili into serving bowls. Sprinkle individual servings with cheese. If desired, serve with lime wedges and tortilla chips.

Nutrition facts per serving: 398 cal., 14 g total fat (6 g sat. fat), 57 mg chol., 1030 mg sodium, 40 g carb., 10 g dietary fiber, 27 g protein.

*Tip: Because chile peppers contain volatile oils that can burn your skin and eyes, avoid direct contact with them as much as possible. When working with chile peppers, wear plastic or rubber gloves. If your bare hands do touch the peppers, wash your hands and nails well with soap and warm water.

chunky BEAN AND CHICKEN CHILI

The crushed tortilla chips added to the chili act as a thickener and give it great whole grain texture.

Start to Finish: 20 minutes
Oven: broil
Makes: 4 servings

- 3 **cups tortilla chips**
- 2 **teaspoons vegetable oil**
- 1 **pound skinless, boneless chicken breasts or thighs, cut into bite-size pieces**
- 2 **19-ounces cans white kidney (cannellini) beans, rinsed and drained**
- 1½ **cups shredded Monterey Jack cheese with jalapeño chile peppers (6 ounces)**
- 1 **4.5-ounce can diced green chile peppers, undrained**
- 1 **14-ounce can reduced-sodium chicken broth**
- ½ **cup water**
  Fresh cilantro (optional)

1 Preheat broiler. Coarsely crush 2 cups of the chips.

2 In a 4- to 5- quart Dutch oven, heat oil over medium-high heat. Add chicken; cook until browned. Add beans, 1 cup of the cheese, chiles, chicken broth, the water, and the 2 cups crushed chips. Bring to boiling; reduce heat. Simmer, uncovered, for 5 minutes, stirring occasionally.

3 Meanwhile, for tortilla crisps, place the remaining 1 cup chips on a baking sheet lined with nonstick foil. Sprinkle with the remaining ½ cup cheese. Broil 6 inches from the heat for 1 to 2 minutes or until cheese is melted and begins to brown. Serve chili with tortilla crisps. If desired, sprinkle with cilantro.

Nutrition facts per serving: 575 cal., 23 g total fat (10 g sat. fat), 111 mg chol., 1172 mg sodium, 52 g carb., 14 g dietary fiber, 55 g protein.

sandwiches
AND PIZZA

Triple-Decker Chicken Clubs, *page 120*

chicken-pesto SANDWICHES

Dine out at home on chicken sandwich wedges just like those served in fancy bistros. Focaccia is available at many bakeries and large supermarkets.

Prep: 30 minutes
Cook: 4 to 5 hours (low)
or 2 to 2½ hours
(high)
Makes: 6 to 8 servings

1 **teaspoon dried Italian seasoning, crushed**

¼ **teaspoon salt**

¼ **teaspoon ground black pepper**

1 **pound skinless, boneless chicken breast halves**

1 **large onion, thinly sliced**

8 **ounces mushrooms, sliced**

2 **cloves garlic, minced**

1 **14.5-ounce can diced tomatoes, undrained**

2 **tablespoons red wine vinegar**

1 **medium yellow summer squash or zucchini, halved lengthwise and sliced ¼ inch thick**

1 **large green, red, or yellow sweet pepper, cut in strips**

⅓ **cup mayonnaise or salad dressing**

2 **tablespoons purchased basil pesto**

1 **9- to 10-inch Italian flatbread (focaccia), cut in half horizontally**

2 **ounces provolone cheese, shredded**

1 In a small bowl, combine Italian seasoning, salt, and black pepper. Rub spice mixture into chicken on all sides with fingers.

2 In a 3½- or 4-quart slow cooker, combine chicken, onion, mushrooms, and garlic. Pour tomatoes and vinegar over mixture in cooker.

3 Cover and cook on low-heat setting for 4 to 5 hours or on high-heat setting for 2 to 2½ hours.

4 If using low-heat setting, turn to high-heat setting. Add squash and sweet pepper. Cover and cook for 30 minutes more.

5 Meanwhile, in a small bowl, combine mayonnaise and pesto. Spread evenly over cut sides of flatbread. Transfer chicken to a cutting board. Thinly slice chicken. Arrange chicken slices on bottom half of bread, pesto side up. Using a slotted spoon, spoon vegetable mixture over chicken. Sprinkle with cheese. Add top half of bread, pesto side down. Cut into wedges.

Nutrition facts per serving: 439 cal., 18 g total fat (4 g sat. fat), 63 mg chol., 770 mg sodium, 43 g carb., 3 g dietary fiber, 29 g protein.

chicken AND HUMMUS PITAS

Prep: 20 minutes
Broil: 12 minutes
Oven: broil
Makes: 4 servings

1   tablespoon olive oil

1   teaspoon lemon juice

¼   teaspoon paprika

    Pinch of salt

    Pinch of ground black
    pepper

2   small skinless, boneless
    chicken breast halves
    (8 to 12 ounces total)

2   large whole wheat pita
    bread rounds, halved

1   7-ounce container
    hummus

¾   cup coarsely chopped
    roma tomatoes

½   cup thinly sliced
    cucumber

⅓   cup low-fat plain yogurt

1 Preheat broiler. In a small bowl, combine oil, lemon juice, paprika, salt, and pepper. Place chicken on the unheated rack of a broiler pan. Brush all sides of the chicken breast halves with the oil mixture. Broil 4 to 5 inches from heat for 12 to 15 minutes or until chicken is no longer pink (170°F), turning once halfway through broiling. Cool slightly; cut into strips.

2 Cut pita rounds in half crosswise; open pita halves to make pockets. Spread hummus inside pita pockets. Stuff pockets with chicken strips, tomatoes, cucumber, and yogurt.

Nutrition facts per serving: 289 cal., 10 g total fat (2 g sat. fat), 34 mg chol., 380 mg sodium, 31 g carb., 5 g dietary fiber, 20 g protein.

greek DELI–STYLE PITAS

Start to Finish: 20 minutes
Makes: 4 servings

¼ **cup low-fat plain yogurt**

2 **teaspoons vinegar**

1 **teaspoon snipped
    fresh dill, or ¼ teaspoon
    dried dill**

½ **teaspoon sugar**

1 **cup thinly sliced
    cucumber**

½ **of a small red onion,
    halved and thinly sliced**

½ **cup chopped roma
    tomatoes**

4 **6-inch whole wheat or
    white pita bread rounds**

10 **ounces thinly sliced
    cooked chicken**

1 In a medium bowl, combine yogurt, vinegar, dill, and sugar. Add cucumber, red onion, and tomatoes. Toss gently to coat. Set aside.

2 Cut pita rounds in half crosswise; open pita halves to make pockets. Line pita pockets with chicken. Spoon the cucumber mixture into pita pockets.

Nutrition facts per serving: 274 cal., 4 g total fat (1 g sat. fat), 40 mg chol., 1204 mg sodium, 45 g carb., 6 g dietary fiber, 18 g protein.

extra-saucy CHICKEN SANDWICHES

With a river of cheddar cheese sauce, this rarebit-style treat is definitely a knife-and-fork kind of sandwich.

Prep: 20 minutes
Cook: 8 to 10 minutes
Makes: 6 servings

2 **tablespoons vegetable oil**

1 **large onion, halved crosswise and thinly sliced**

2 **pounds skinless, boneless chicken breast halves, cut into bite-size strips**

1 **14- to 16-ounce jar cheddar cheese pasta sauce**

2 **tablespoons Worcestershire sauce**

12 **slices marbled rye bread, toasted**

1 **tomato, sliced**

12 **slices bacon, crisp-cooked and drained (optional)**

1 In a very large skillet, heat 1 tablespoon of the oil over medium-high heat. Add onion and half of the chicken. Cook and stir for 4 to 5 minutes or until chicken is no longer pink. Transfer to a medium bowl. Add remaining oil and remaining chicken to skillet. Cook for 4 to 5 minutes more or until chicken is no longer pink. Return chicken and onion mixture to skillet. Add pasta sauce and Worcestershire sauce. Heat through.

2 To serve, spoon chicken and sauce mixture over 6 bread slices. Top with tomato and, if desired, bacon. Top with remaining 6 bread slices.

Nutrition facts per serving: 491 cal., 18 g total fat (5 g sat. fat), 114 mg chol., 1084 mg sodium, 38 g carb., 4 g dietary fiber, 43 g protein.

triple-decker CHICKEN CLUBS

You can build a smaller version of this classic double-decker sandwich for little hands and mouths.

Start to Finish: 20 minutes
Makes: 4 servings

⅔ **cup light mayonnaise or salad dressing**

¼ **teaspoon ground black pepper**

2 **6-ounce packages refrigerated cooked chicken breast strips, chopped**

1 **cup chopped, cored apple**

8 **lettuce leaves**

12 **slices whole wheat bread, toasted***

1 **large tomato, sliced**

8 **slices packaged ready-to-serve cooked bacon**

In a large bowl, combine mayonnaise and pepper. Stir in chicken and apple. To assemble sandwiches, place 1 lettuce leaf on 4 of the toasted bread slices. Top lettuce with tomato slices and bacon. Top bacon with another slice of bread. Top with remaining lettuce leaves; spoon chicken mixture atop lettuce. Top with remaining bread slices.

Nutrition facts per serving: 504 cal., 24 g total fat (5 g sat. fat), 84 mg chol., 1349 mg sodium, 44 g carb., 6 g dietary fiber, 32 g protein.

*Tip: For smaller sandwiches, use only 8 slices bread and 4 lettuce leaves. Assemble sandwiches as directed, omitting the middle layers of bread and lettuce.

chicken-spinach CALZONES

Prep: 20 minutes
Bake: 20 minutes
Oven: 375°F
Makes: 8 servings

3 **cups chopped cooked chicken or turkey**

2½ **cups coarsely chopped fresh spinach**

1½ **cups shredded mozzarella cheese (6 ounces)**

1 **8-ounce can tomato sauce**

1 **teaspoon dried Italian seasoning, crushed**

2 **teaspoon bottled minced garlic**

2 **13.8-ounce packages refrigerated pizza dough**

Milk

Grated Parmesan or Romano cheese (optional)

Pizza or pasta sauce, warmed (optional)

1 Preheat oven to 375°F. Line 1 very large or 2 smaller baking sheets with parchment paper. In a large bowl, combine chicken, spinach, mozzarella cheese, tomato sauce, Italian seasoning, and garlic. Unroll pizza dough. Cut each into 4 rectangles. Gently stretch each rectangle to a 6-inch square.

2 Place about ½ cup of the chicken mixture onto half of each square, leaving about ½-inch border around edges. Fold dough over filling, forming a rectangle. Press edges with a fork to seal edges. Prick tops; brush with milk. Place on prepared baking sheet or sheets.

3 If desired, sprinkle tops of calzones with Parmesan cheese. Bake for about 20 minutes or until golden brown. If desired, serve with pizza sauce.

Nutrition facts per serving: 378 cal., 13 g total fat (4 g sat. fat), 58 mg chol., 659 mg sodium, 40 g carb., 2 g dietary fiber, 27 g protein.

chicken SALAD SANDWICHES

Start to Finish: 25 minutes
Makes: 4 servings

1   cup chopped cooked
    chicken breast (5 ounces)

⅓   cup chopped cored apple
    or finely chopped celery

1   hard-cooked egg, peeled
    and chopped

2   tablespoons low-fat plain
    yogurt

2   tablespoons light
    mayonnaise or salad
    dressing

⅛   teaspoon salt

⅛   teaspoon ground black
    pepper

8   slices whole wheat bread

4   leaf lettuce or romaine
    lettuce leaves

1   medium tomato, thinly
    sliced

½   of a small cucumber,
    thinly sliced (about
    ¾ cup)

1 In a medium bowl, stir together chicken, apple, and egg. Add yogurt, mayonnaise, salt, and pepper; stir to combine.*

2 Top half of the bread slices with a lettuce leaf. Then add tomato slices, cucumber slices, and some of the chicken mixture to each. Add the remaining bread slices on top. Cut each sandwich in half.

Nutrition facts per serving: 248 cal., 7 g total fat (2 g sat. fat), 86 mg chol., 447 mg sodium, 28 g carb., 5 g dietary fiber, 18 g protein.

*Tip: If desired, cover and chill the chicken mixture for up to 4 hours before using.

mustard CHICKEN SALAD SANDWICHES

Prep: 25 minutes
Chill: 1 hour
Makes: 4 servings

¼ **cup mayonnaise**

2 **tablespoons creamy Dijon-style mustard blend**

2 **tablespoons coarse-grain brown mustard**

2½ **cups chopped cooked chicken or turkey**

¼ **cup finely chopped celery**

¼ **cup thinly sliced scallions**

2 **tablespoons pine nuts, toasted**

1 **tablespoon snipped fresh parsley**

1 **tablespoon drained and finely chopped oil-packed dried tomatoes**

Salt and ground black pepper

4 **croissants**

1 For dressing, in a small bowl stir together mayonnaise and mustards.

2 In a medium bowl, combine chicken, celery, scallions, pine nuts, parsley, and tomatoes. Season to taste with salt and pepper. Pour dressing over chicken mixture; toss to coat. Cover and chill for 1 to 4 hours.

3 Serve chicken salad as sandwich filling on croissants.

Nutrition facts per serving: 556 cal., 34 g total fat (10 g sat. fat), 121 mg chol., 882 mg sodium, 29 g carb., 2 g dietary fiber, 31 g protein.

bbq ranch CHICKEN SANDWICHES

Prep: 15 minutes
Bake: 7 minutes
Oven: 450°F
Makes: 4 servings

- 1 **10-ounce (12-inch) Italian bread shell**
- **Nonstick cooking spray**
- 1½ **cups shredded Colby-Jack cheese (6 ounces)**
- 1 **cup cooked shredded chicken**
- 2 **tablespoons barbecue sauce**
- 6 **slices packaged ready-to-serve cooked bacon**
- 1½ **cups shredded lettuce**
- 2 **tablespoons finely chopped sweet onion**
- 1 **tablespoon bottled ranch salad dressing**
- 1 **medium tomato, sliced**

1 Preheat oven to 450°F. Place bread shell on baking sheet, bottom side up. Coat bread shell with nonstick cooking spray. With pizza cutter, cut bread in half. Sprinkle cheese evenly over bread halves. In a small bowl, combine chicken and barbecue sauce. Top one bread half with chicken mixture and the bacon slices.

2 Bake for 7 to 9 minutes or until cheese melts and bacon is crisp. Cool on baking sheet for 2 minutes. Meanwhile, in a small bowl combine lettuce, onion, and ranch salad dressing.

3 To serve, cut each half into quarters to make 8 wedges. Spoon lettuce mixture evenly over wedges with chicken. Top with tomato slices. Invert remaining wedges over toppings.

Nutrition facts per serving: 608 cal., 27 g total fat (11 g sat. fat), 86 mg chol., 1196 mg sodium, 56 g carb., 1 g dietary fiber, 35 g protein.

cobb SALAD WRAPS

Avoid last-minute lunchtime hassle by preparing and chilling the ingredients the night before. In the morning, you'll be ready to wrap and roll.

Start to Finish: 30 minutes
Makes: 8 servings

- 1 cup blue cheese salad dressing
- 8 8- to 10-inch whole wheat or Southwest-flavor flour tortillas
- 8 romaine lettuce leaves, ribs removed
- 8 slices bacon, crisp-cooked and drained
- 4 scallions, cut into thin strips
- 4 roma tomatoes, seeded and cut into thin wedges
- 1 cup shredded mozzarella cheese (4 ounces)
- 1 pound cooked chicken, shredded

Spread some of the salad dressing over 1 side of each tortilla. Top each with lettuce, bacon, scallions, tomatoes, cheese, and shredded chicken. Roll up tightly. Serve immediately or wrap each roll in plastic wrap and chill in the refrigerator for 2 to 4 hours.

Nutrition facts per serving: 404 cal., 26 g total fat (7 g sat. fat), 69 mg chol., 734 mg sodium, 17 g carb., 10 g dietary fiber, 26 g protein.

basil CHICKEN WRAPS

Start to Finish: 15 minutes
Oven: 350°F
Makes: 4 servings

4   8- or 9-inch plain flour
    tortillas or tomato- or
    spinach-flavored flour
    tortillas

½   cup Basil Mayonnaise*
    Fresh basil leaves

12 ounces thinly sliced
    cooked chicken or
    turkey, cut into thin
    strips

½   cup roasted red sweet
    peppers, cut into thin
    strips

1 Preheat oven to 350°F. Place the stack of tortillas on foil; wrap tightly. Heat for about 10 minutes or until warm.

2 Spread Basil Mayonnaise onto warm tortillas. Arrange basil leaves, chicken, and sweet peppers on tortillas. Fold up bottoms; roll up.

*__Basil Mayonnaise:__ Stir together ½ cup low-fat mayonnaise or salad dressing, 1 tablespoon snipped fresh basil, and 1 small clove garlic, minced. If desired, stir in ⅛ teaspoon cayenne pepper. Makes about ½ cup.

Nutrition facts per serving: 366 cal., 15 g total fat (3 g sat. fat), 44 mg chol., 1330 mg sodium, 37 g carb., 2 g dietary fiber, 21 g protein.

thai CHICKEN-BROCCOLI WRAPS

Start to Finish: 25 minutes
Makes: 6 servings

12 ounces skinless, boneless chicken breast strips for stir-frying
¼ teaspoon garlic salt
⅛ teaspoon ground black pepper
2 cups packaged shredded broccoli (broccoli slaw mix)
¼ teaspoon ground ginger
3 10-inch whole wheat flour tortillas, warmed**
Peanut Sauce*

1 Sprinkle chicken strips with garlic salt and pepper. Coat a large nonstick skillet with nonstick cooking spray. Preheat skillet over medium-high heat. Add seasoned chicken; cook and stir for 2 to 3 minutes or until chicken is no longer pink. Remove chicken from skillet; keep warm. Add broccoli and ginger to skillet. Cook and stir for 2 to 3 minutes or until vegetables are crisp-tender.

2 Spread tortillas with Peanut Sauce.* Top with chicken strips and vegetable mixture. Roll up tortillas. Cut each wrap in half. Serve immediately.

***Peanut Sauce:** In a small saucepan, combine 3 tablespoons creamy peanut butter; 2 tablespoons water; 1 tablespoon reduced-sodium soy sauce; 1 clove garlic, minced; and ¼ teaspoon ground ginger. Heat over very low heat until melted and smooth, whisking constantly.

Nutrition facts per serving: 191 cal., 6 g total fat (1 g sat. fat), 33 mg chol., 460 mg sodium, 16 g carb., 2 g dietary fiber, 18 g protein.

****Tip:** To warm tortillas, preheat oven to 350°F. Wrap tortillas tightly in foil. Heat in the oven for about 10 minutes or until heated through.

spicy CHICKEN PO' BOYS WITH RANCH SLAW

This po' boy is made from spice-crusted chicken thighs that turn a crispy black on the outside when sautéed. The coleslaw provides a cooling counterpoint to the spicy chicken.

Prep: 25 minutes
Chill: 1 hour
Makes: 8 servings

3 cups packaged shredded cabbage with carrot (coleslaw mix)

3 tablespoons bottled ranch salad dressing

1 teaspoon ground chipotle chile pepper or chili powder

½ teaspoon sugar

½ teaspoon kosher salt or salt

½ teaspoon garlic powder

½ teaspoon ground cumin

2 pounds skinless, boneless chicken thighs

1 tablespoon olive oil

8 individual ciabatta or French rolls, split

1 For slaw, in a medium bowl combine coleslaw mix and ranch salad dressing. Cover and chill for 1 hour.

2 For chicken, in a shallow dish combine chipotle chile pepper, sugar, salt, garlic powder, and cumin. Sprinkle both sides of each chicken thigh with spice mixture, coating lightly.

3 In a large nonstick skillet, heat oil over medium-high heat. Add chicken; cook for 10 to 14 minutes or until chicken is lightly blackened and no longer pink (180°F), turning once.

4 To serve, slice chicken thighs and place on bottom halves of split rolls. Top with slaw and roll tops.

Nutrition facts per serving: 504 cal., 14 g total fat (3 g sat. fat), 92 mg chol., 941 mg sodium, 59 g carb., 4 g dietary fiber, 33 g protein.

tex-mex SLOPPY JOES

Start to Finish: 30 minutes
Makes: 8 servings

1 **pound ground chicken breast or turkey breast**

2 **medium onions, chopped**

1 **medium green sweet pepper, seeded and chopped**

½ **cup loose-pack frozen whole kernel corn**

2 **large cloves garlic, minced**

1 **fresh jalapeño chile pepper, seeded (if desired) and finely chopped***

1 **teaspoon chili powder**

1 **teaspoon ground cumin**

1 **teaspoon dried oregano, crushed, or 1 tablespoon snipped fresh oregano**

¾ **cup ketchup**

4 **teaspoons Worcestershire sauce**

8 **whole wheat hamburger buns**

Dill pickle slices (optional)

1 In a large nonstick skillet, combine ground chicken breast, onions, sweet pepper, corn, garlic, chile pepper, chili powder, cumin, and oregano. Cook over medium heat until chicken is no longer pink and onions are tender, stirring frequently. Stir in ketchup and Worcestershire sauce; heat through.

2 Divide chicken mixture among buns. If desired, top with pickle slices.

Nutrition facts per serving: 208 cal., 6 g total fat (0 g sat. fat), 0 mg chol., 453 mg sodium, 26 g carb., 4 g dietary fiber, 13 g protein.

*Tip: Because chile peppers contain volatile oils that can burn your skin and eyes, avoid direct contact with them as much as possible. When working with chile peppers, wear plastic or rubber gloves. If your bare hands do touch the peppers, wash your hands and nails well with soap and warm water.

southwest CHICKEN BURGERS

Start to Finish: 30 minutes
Makes: 4 servings

½ **cup shredded zucchini**

2 **tablespoons canned diced green chile peppers, drained**

½ **teaspoon ground cumin**

½ **teaspoon salt**

½ **teaspoon ground black pepper**

1 **pound ground chicken or turkey**

1 **tablespoon olive oil or cooking oil**

½ **cup salsa**

1 **scallion, chopped (2 tablespoons)**

2 **tablespoons snipped fresh cilantro**

1 **tablespoon low-fat plain yogurt**

4 **7- or 8-inch flour tortillas, or 4 hamburger buns, split and toasted**

Lettuce leaves

❶ Combine zucchini, green chiles, cumin, salt, and pepper. Add ground chicken; mix well. Shape chicken mixture into four ½-inch-thick patties.

❷ In a large skillet, cook patties in hot oil over medium heat for about 10 minutes or until no longer pink (165°F), turning once.

❸ Meanwhile, combine salsa, scallion, cilantro, and yogurt. Place each burger on the upper half of a tortilla. Add lettuce and salsa mixture. Fold the bottom half over burger; fold the sides to the center, overlapping slightly. (If using hamburger buns, line bottoms of the toasted buns with lettuce leaves; add the burger, salsa mixture, and bun tops.)

Nutrition facts per serving: 323 cal., 15 g total fat (1 g sat. fat), 0 mg chol., 726 mg sodium, 23 g carb., 2 g dietary fiber, 23 g protein.

chicken DINNER BURGERS

Prep: 15 minutes
Cook: 12 minutes
Makes: 4 servings

1 egg, lightly beaten
½ teaspoon salt
¼ teaspoon ground black
   pepper
1 pound ground chicken or
   ground turkey
¼ cup fine dry bread crumbs
1 tablespoon olive oil
¼ cup barbecue sauce
4 slices Texas toast or other
   thick-sliced bread
   Prepared coleslaw or
   grated jicama (optional)
   Pickle slices (optional)

1 In a medium bowl, combine egg, salt, and pepper. Add chicken and bread crumbs; mix well. Shape the chicken mixture into four ¾-inch-thick patties.

2 In a large nonstick skillet, cook patties over medium heat in hot oil for about 10 minutes or until an instant-read thermometer inserted into the thickest part of the burger registers 165°F, turning once halfway through cooking time. Brush patties on each side with barbecue sauce. Cook for 1 minute more on each side to glaze.

3 Place burgers on slices of Texas toast. If desired, top with coleslaw and pickle slices.

Nutrition facts per serving: 371 cal., 17 g total fat (1 g sat. fat), 103 mg chol., 912 mg sodium, 27 g carb., 0 g dietary fiber, 28 g protein.

To Broil: Place patties on the unheated rack of a broiler pan. Broil 4 to 5 inches from the heat for about 10 minutes or until an instant-read thermometer inserted into the thickest part of the burger registers 165°F, turning once halfway through cooking time. Brush patties on each side with barbecue sauce. Cook for 1 minute more on each side to glaze.

chicken CAESAR SALAD PIZZA

Start to Finish: 20 minutes
Oven: 450°F
Makes: 4 servings

1 **12-inch whole wheat Italian bread shell**

½ **cup shredded reduced-fat mozzarella cheese (2 ounces)**

2 **cups packaged European mixed salad greens**

2 **cups grilled chicken breast cut into thin strips**

2 **medium roma tomatoes, chopped**

¼ **cup quartered and thinly sliced red onion**

2 **tablespoons halved pitted kalamata olives**

3 **tablespoons bottled light Caesar salad dressing**

2 **tablespoons crumbled reduced-fat feta cheese**

1 Preheat oven to 450°F. Sprinkle bread shell with mozzarella cheese. Place shell directly on middle oven rack. Bake about 5 minutes or until cheese is melted.

2 Meanwhile, in a large bowl, toss together salad greens, chicken, tomatoes, onion, and olives. Add salad dressing; toss to coat. Remove bread shell from oven; immediately top with salad greens mixture. Sprinkle with feta cheese. Cut into wedges. Serve immediately.

Nutrition facts per serving: 388 cal., 11 g total fat (3 g sat. fat), 70 mg chol., 830 mg sodium, 39 g carb., 6 g dietary fiber, 35 g protein.

buffalo CHICKEN PIZZAS

Start to Finish: 20 minutes
Oven: 450°F
Makes: 4 servings

4 pita bread rounds
¼ cup bottled blue cheese
   salad dressing
1 9-ounce package
   refrigerated Southwest-
   flavor cooked chicken
   breast strips, cut into
   bite-size pieces
2 stalks celery, cut into thin
   strips
¼ cup blue cheese crumbles
   Bottled hot pepper sauce
   or buffalo wing sauce
   (optional)

1 Preheat oven to 450°F. Place pita rounds on baking sheet. Brush with blue cheese dressing. Top with chicken and celery strips.

2 Bake, uncovered, for about 10 minutes or until heated through and pitas are crisp. Sprinkle with blue cheese crumbles. If desired, pass hot pepper sauce.

Nutrition facts per serving: 353 cal., 13 g total fat (4 g sat. fat), 52 mg chol., 1171 mg sodium, 36 g carb., 2 g dietary fiber, 22 g protein.

alfredo CHICKEN PITA PIZZAS

Start to Finish: 20 minutes
Oven: 450°F
Makes: 4 servings

- **4 large pita bread rounds**
- **½ cup refrigerated Alfredo pasta sauce**
- **1 6-ounce package refrigerated cooked chicken breast strips**
- **½ cup roasted red sweet peppers, cut into thin strips**
- **¼ cup sliced scallions**
- **1 cup finely shredded Italian cheese blend**

Preheat oven to 450°F. Place pita bread rounds on a large baking sheet. Bake for 6 to 8 minutes or until light brown. Spread tops of pitas with Alfredo pasta sauce. Top with chicken breast strips, roasted sweet peppers, scallions, and cheese. Bake for 6 to 8 minutes more or until cheese melts and toppings are heated through.

Nutrition facts per serving: 387 cal., 15 g total fat (8 g sat. fat), 65 mg chol., 1123 mg sodium, 39 g carb., 2 g dietary fiber, 24 g protein.

barbecued CHICKEN PIZZA

Prep: 20 minutes
Bake: 15 minutes
Oven: 425°F
Makes: 6 servings

1 12-inch purchased Italian flatbread (focaccia) or Italian bread shell, or one 10-ounce package refrigerated pizza dough

2 cups shredded cooked chicken

½ cup bottled barbecue sauce

6 ounces shredded Monterey Jack cheese (1½ cups)

¼ cup finely chopped spinach

1 Preheat oven to 425°F. Place flatbread or bread shell on 14-inch pizza pan. (Or, lightly grease a 15x10x1-inch baking pan. Unroll the pizza dough onto greased pan, using your hands to press dough into a 14x9-inch rectangle; build up the edges slightly. Bake pizza dough for 5 minutes. Remove from oven.)

2 In a bowl, combine chicken and barbecue sauce; toss to coat. Spread chicken mixture evenly over the crust. Sprinkle with cheese and spinach.

3 Bake for about 10 minutes or until crust edge is lightly browned. Cut flatbread or bread shell into wedges. (Or, cut rectangular pizza into 6 squares; cut each square diagonally into 2 triangles.)

Nutrition facts per serving: 405 cal., 18 g total fat (8 g sat. fat), 66 mg chol., 360 mg sodium, 35 g carb., 3 g dietary fiber, 27 g protein.

fresh TOMATO AND CHICKEN PIZZA

Start to Finish: 23 minutes
Oven: 425°F
Makes: 4 servings

1 **tablespoon cornmeal**

1 **10-ounce package refrigerated pizza dough**

3 **medium roma tomatoes, thinly sliced**

4 **ounces cooked chicken, cut into 1-inch cubes**

3 **tablespoons snipped fresh basil**

¼ **teaspoon coarsely ground black pepper**

1 **cup shredded reduced-fat mozzarella cheese (4 ounces)**

1 Preheat oven to 425°F. Coat a 12-inch pizza pan with nonstick cooking spray. Sprinkle cornmeal over bottom of pan. Press refrigerated dough into prepared pan, building up edges. Arrange tomato slices and chicken cubes on the dough. Sprinkle with basil and pepper. Sprinkle mozzarella cheese on top.

2 Bake for 13 to 18 minutes or until cheese is bubbly.

Nutrition facts per serving: 281 cal., 8 g total fat (3 g sat. fat), 39 mg chol., 420 mg sodium, 31 g carb., 2 g dietary fiber, 20 g protein.

chicken TACO PIZZAS

Start to Finish: 25 minutes
Oven: 425°F
Makes: 4 servings

2 whole wheat pita bread
   rounds, split horizontally

1 teaspoon olive oil or
   canola oil

2 5-ounce cans no-salt-
   added chunk chicken
   breast, drained

¼ cup bottled salsa

1 cup shredded reduced-fat
   Monterey Jack and/or
   cheddar cheese
   (4 ounces)

1½ cups shredded lettuce

⅔ cup halved grape
   tomatoes or chopped
   tomato

   Light Sour Cream Drizzle*

1 Preheat oven to 425°F. Place pita bread pieces, cut sides up, on an ungreased baking sheet. Lightly brush cut sides of each piece with oil. Bake for about 4 minutes or until lightly browned and crisp.

2 Meanwhile, in a small bowl, stir together drained chicken and salsa. Evenly spoon chicken mixture over pita bread pieces. Sprinkle with cheese.

3 Bake for about 5 minutes more or until chicken is heated through and cheese melts.

4 To serve, top with lettuce and grape tomatoes. Drizzle with Light Sour Cream Drizzle.

*Light Sour Cream Drizzle: In a small bowl, stir together ¼ cup light sour cream and 1 to 2 teaspoons fat-free milk. If desired, transfer mixture to a small resealable plastic bag. Snip off one corner and squeeze onto pizzas.

Nutrition facts per serving: 248 cal., 9 g total fat (4 g sat. fat), 69 mg chol., 483 mg sodium, 22 g carb., 3 g dietary fiber, 23 g protein.

baked
AND ROASTED

Oven-Barbecued Chicken, *page 166*

sweet-and-sour BAKED CHICKEN

Baking makes classic sweet-and-sour chicken easier to make. For a family-size version, serve this with hot cooked rice.

Prep: 25 minutes
Bake: 30 minutes
Oven: 350°F
Makes: 4 servings

8   medium skinless, boneless chicken breast halves (about 2½ pounds)

    Salt and ground black pepper

1   tablespoon cooking oil

1   20-ounce can pineapple chunks (juice pack)

½   cup canned jellied cranberry sauce

2   tablespoons cornstarch

2   tablespoons packed brown sugar

2   tablespoons rice vinegar or cider vinegar

2   tablespoons frozen orange juice concentrate, thawed

2   tablespoons dry sherry, chicken broth, or water

2   tablespoons soy sauce

¼   teaspoon ground ginger

1   medium green sweet pepper, cut into bite-size strips

1 Preheat oven to 350°F. Sprinkle chicken lightly with salt and pepper. In a large skillet, heat oil over medium-high heat. Add chicken and cook for about 2 minutes on each side or until brown. Transfer chicken to a 2-quart rectangular baking dish. Drain pineapple well, reserving ⅓ cup juice. Spoon pineapple chunks evenly over chicken in dish.

2 For sauce, in a medium saucepan whisk together the reserved pineapple juice, the cranberry sauce, cornstarch, brown sugar, vinegar, orange juice concentrate, sherry, soy sauce, and ginger. Cook and stir over medium heat until thickened and bubbly. Pour over chicken and pineapple in dish.

3 Bake, covered, for 25 minutes. Uncover and add sweet pepper strips, stirring gently to coat with sauce. Bake, uncovered, for about 5 minutes more or until chicken is no longer pink (170°F).

Nutrition facts per serving: 368 cal., 6 g total fat (1 g sat. fat), 82 mg chol., 589 mg sodium, 41 g carb., 2 g dietary fiber, 35 g protein.

baked HERBED CHICKEN

Prep: 20 minutes
Bake: 25 minutes
Oven: 375°F
Makes: 4 servings

4   skinless, boneless chicken
    breast halves
    Salt and coarsely ground
    black pepper
½   of an 8-ounce package
    cream cheese, softened
¼   cup finely chopped red or
    green sweet pepper
½   teaspoon snipped fresh
    rosemary or tarragon, or
    ¼ teaspoon dried
    rosemary or tarragon,
    crushed
1   tablespoon olive oil
1   tablespoon snipped fresh
    chives

1 Preheat oven to 375°F. Place each chicken breast half between pieces of plastic wrap. Using the flat side of a meat mallet, pound lightly to about a ⅛-inch thickness. Remove plastic wrap.

2 Season chicken with salt and pepper. Top each chicken piece with 2 tablespoons of the cream cheese and 1 tablespoon of the sweet pepper. Sprinkle with rosemary. Fold in the sides. Roll up, pressing the edges to seal. Secure the rolls with wooden toothpicks, if necessary.

3 In a large skillet, cook chicken rolls in hot oil over medium-high heat for about 4 minutes or until lightly browned, turning to brown all sides. Remove to a 2-quart square baking dish. Sprinkle with pepper. Bake, uncovered, for 25 to 30 minutes or until chicken is no longer pink (170°F).

4 Sprinkle with snipped chives.

Nutrition facts per serving: 292 cal., 15 g total fat (7 g sat. fat), 113 mg chol., 307 mg sodium, 1 g carb., 0 g dietary fiber, 35 g protein.

chicken WITH POBLANO SALSA

Here the dark green poblano, best known for its role in the Mexican classic chiles rellenos, brings on a medium to hot, rich flavor. If you can't find poblanos, use Anaheim peppers instead.

Prep: 30 minutes
Bake: 20 minutes plus
　　　 15 minutes
Oven: 450°F/375°F
Makes: 4 servings

1　**large fresh poblano chile pepper***

1　**large clove garlic**

⅓　**cup fine dry bread crumbs**

1　**tablespoon chili powder**

1　**teaspoon ground cumin**

4　**skinless, boneless chicken breast halves (1¼ to 1½ pounds total)**

1　**egg, beaten**

⅔　**cup chopped tomato (1 medium)**

½　**cup chopped tomatillo or tomato**

¼　**cup chopped onion**

2　**tablespoons snipped fresh cilantro**

1 Preheat oven to 450°F. To roast poblano pepper and garlic, quarter the pepper, removing seeds and membranes. Place pepper pieces and unpeeled garlic clove on a foil-lined baking sheet. Bake, uncovered, for 20 to 25 minutes or until the skin on pepper pieces is charred. Remove garlic. Bring up the edges of foil and seal around the pepper pieces. Let stand for 20 minutes to steam. Peel pepper pieces and garlic. Chop pepper; mash garlic. Lower oven to 375°F.

2 Meanwhile, coat a 2-quart rectangular baking dish with nonstick cooking spray. In a shallow dish, combine the bread crumbs, chili powder, and cumin. Dip chicken into egg; dip into bread crumb mixture to coat. Arrange chicken in baking dish. Bake, uncovered, for 15 to 20 minutes or until chicken is tender and no longer pink (170°F).

3 For salsa, in a medium bowl combine the poblano pepper, garlic, tomato, tomatillo, onion, and cilantro. To serve, slice chicken and spoon salsa over slices.

Nutrition facts per serving: 233 cal., 5 g total fat (1 g sat. fat), 135 mg chol., 294 mg sodium, 11 g carb., 2 g dietary fiber, 36 g protein.

***Tip:** Because chile peppers contain volatile oils that can burn your skin and eyes, avoid direct contact with them as much as possible. When working with chile peppers, wear plastic or rubber gloves. If your bare hands do touch the peppers, wash your hands and nails well with soap and warm water.

peppered CHICKEN IN MARSALA SAUCE

Coated with ground pepper, this chicken, in a simple Marsala and mushroom sauce, boasts a big flavor you won't soon forget.

Prep: 20 minutes
Bake: 35 minutes
Oven: 425°F
Makes: 6 servings

- **6 bone-in chicken breast halves (about 3½ pounds total)**
- **2 teaspoons olive oil or cooking oil**
- **1 teaspoon coarsely ground black pepper**
- **¼ teaspoon salt**
- **2 cups sliced fresh mushrooms**
- **2 tablespoons butter**
- **3 tablespoons all-purpose flour**
- **¼ teaspoon salt**
- **1¼ cups reduced-sodium chicken broth**
- **¼ cup dry Marsala**
- **Coarsely ground black pepper (optional)**

1 Preheat oven to 425°F. Skin chicken. Brush chicken with oil; sprinkle the 1 teaspoon pepper and ¼ teaspoon salt over chicken. Arrange chicken in a 15x10x1-inch baking pan. Bake, uncovered, for 35 to 40 minutes or until chicken is tender and no longer pink (170°F).

2 Meanwhile, for sauce, in a medium saucepan cook mushrooms in hot butter until tender. Stir in flour and ¼ teaspoon salt. Add broth and Marsala. Cook and stir over medium heat until thickened and bubbly; cook and stir for 1 minute more. Pass sauce with chicken. If desired, sprinkle with additional pepper.

Nutrition facts per serving: 255 cal., 9 g total fat (3 g sat. fat), 95 mg chol., 465 mg sodium, 5 g carb., 0 g dietary fiber, 36 g protein.

crispy nuggets WITH
HONEY-MUSTARD DIP

Prep: 20 minutes
Bake: 10 minutes
Oven: 425°F
Makes: 4 servings

- ½ **cup low-fat mayonnaise**
- 4 **teaspoons Dijon-style mustard**
- 1 **tablespoon honey**
- 1 **pound skinless, boneless chicken breast halves**
- ¼ **cup all-purpose flour**
- 1 **teaspoon dried parsley flakes**
- ½ **teaspoon poultry seasoning**
- ⅛ **teaspoon salt**
  Pinch of ground black pepper
- 1 **egg, beaten**
- 2 **tablespoons milk**
- 30 **wheat crackers or rich round crackers, finely crushed (1¼ cups)**

① Preheat oven to 425°F. For honey-mustard dip, in a small bowl stir together mayonnaise, mustard, and honey. Cover and chill until serving time.

② Cut chicken into 1½-inch pieces. In a plastic bag, combine flour, parsley flakes, poultry seasoning, salt, and pepper. Add chicken pieces, a few at a time, to the flour mixture. Close the bag; shake to coat chicken pieces.

③ In a bowl, stir together egg and milk. Place crushed crackers in another bowl. Dip coated chicken pieces, a few at a time, into the egg mixture. Roll the pieces in crackers. Place in a single layer on a large ungreased baking sheet. Bake for 10 to 12 minutes or until chicken is no longer pink.

④ Serve with honey-mustard dip.

Nutrition facts per serving: 354 cal., 10 g total fat (2 g sat. fat), 126 mg chol., 637 mg sodium, 34 g carb., 2 g dietary fiber, 31 g protein.

tortilla-crusted CHICKEN

Prep: 10 minutes
Bake: 25 minutes
Oven: 375°F
Makes: 4 servings

1 cup finely crushed multigrain tortilla chips

½ teaspoon dried oregano, crushed

¼ teaspoon ground cumin

¼ teaspoon ground black pepper

1 egg

4 skinless, boneless chicken breast halves (about 1¼ pounds total)

Shredded romaine lettuce (optional)

Purchased salsa (optional)

Avocado slices (optional)

1 Preheat oven to 375°F. Coat a 15x10x1-inch baking pan with nonstick cooking spray. In a shallow dish, combine tortilla chips, oregano, cumin, and pepper. Place egg in another shallow dish; beat lightly. Dip chicken in beaten egg, then coat with tortilla chip mixture.

2 Arrange chicken in the prepared baking pan. Bake for about 25 minutes or until chicken is no longer pink (170°F). If desired, serve chicken on a bed of shredded romaine with salsa and avocado slices.

Nutrition facts per serving: 230 cal., 6 g total fat (1 g sat. fat), 135 mg chol., 143 mg sodium, 7 g carb., 1 g dietary fiber, 35 g protein.

chicken ALFREDO

Prep: 25 minutes
Bake: 15 minutes
Oven: 350°F
Makes: 6 servings

6 **medium skinless, boneless chicken breast halves**

Salt and ground black pepper

1 **tablespoon cooking oil**

1 **cup whipping cream**

4 **ounces Asiago or Parmesan cheese, finely shredded (1 cup)**

⅓ **cup drained roasted red sweet peppers, cut into thin strips**

3 **tablespoons finely shredded fresh basil**

1 Preheat oven to 350°F. Sprinkle chicken with salt and pepper. In a 12-inch skillet, brown chicken breasts in hot oil for about 10 minutes, turning to brown evenly. Transfer chicken to a 3-quart rectangular baking dish; set aside.

2 For sauce, in a medium saucepan beat whipping cream with a wire whisk or rotary beater for 1 to 2 minutes or until thickened. Heat over medium heat until just simmering. Reduce heat to medium-low. Gradually whisk in cheese until melted.

3 Pour sauce over chicken breasts in dish; top with red peppers. Bake, uncovered, for 15 to 20 minutes or until chicken is no longer pink (170°F). Sprinkle with basil.

Nutrition facts per serving: 418 cal., 27 g total fat (15 g sat. fat), 162 mg chol., 353 mg sodium, 2 g carb., 0 g dietary fiber, 41 g protein.

classic CHICKEN KIEV

Prep: 20 minutes
Chill: 1 hour
Bake: 15 minutes
Oven: 400°F
Makes: 4 servings

- 1 **tablespoon chopped scallion**
- 1 **tablespoon snipped fresh parsley**
- 1 **clove garlic, minced**
- ½ **of 1 stick of butter, chilled**
- 1 **egg, beaten**
- 1 **tablespoon water**
- ¼ **cup all-purpose flour**
- ½ **cup fine dry bread crumbs**
- 4 **skinless, boneless chicken breast halves (1¼ to 1½ pounds total)**
- **Salt and ground black pepper**
- 1 **tablespoon butter**
- 1 **tablespoon cooking oil**

1 In a small bowl, combine scallion, parsley, and garlic. Cut the chilled butter into four 2½x½-inch sticks. In a shallow bowl, stir together egg and water. Place flour in another shallow bowl. Place bread crumbs in another shallow bowl. Set all three bowls aside.

2 Place each chicken breast half between pieces of plastic wrap. Using the flat side of a meat mallet, pound chicken lightly into rectangles about ⅛ inch thick. Remove plastic wrap. Sprinkle with salt and pepper. Divide the scallion mixture among chicken pieces. Place a butter stick in center of each chicken piece. Fold in the side edges; roll up from bottom edge.

3 Coat chicken rolls with flour. Dip in the egg mixture; coat with bread crumbs. Dip in egg mixture again; coat with additional bread crumbs. (Coat ends well to seal in butter.) Place coated chicken rolls in a 2-quart rectangular baking dish. Cover and chill for 1 to 24 hours.

4 Preheat oven to 400°F. In a large skillet, melt the 1 tablespoon butter over medium-high heat; add oil. Add chilled chicken rolls. Cook about 5 minutes or until golden brown, turning to brown all sides. Return rolls to baking dish. Bake, uncovered, for 15 to 18 minutes or until chicken is no longer pink (170°F). To serve, spoon any drippings over rolls.

Nutrition facts per serving: 377 cal., 22 g total fat (11 g sat. fat), 160 mg chol., 499 mg sodium, 13 g carb., 1 g dietary fiber, 30 g protein.

sesame CHICKEN

Dipped in teriyaki sauce and coated with sesame seeds, this no-fuss chicken brings home the flavors of the East.

Prep: 15 minutes
Bake: 45 minutes
Oven: 400°F
Makes: 4 servings

- **4 bone-in chicken breast halves (about 2½ pounds total)**
- **3 tablespoons sesame seeds**
- **3 tablespoons all-purpose flour**
- **¼ teaspoon salt**
- **¼ teaspoon cayenne pepper**
- **3 tablespoons reduced-sodium teriyaki sauce**
- **1 tablespoon butter or margarine, melted**

1 Preheat oven to 400°F. Skin chicken. In a large plastic bag, combine sesame seeds, flour, salt, and cayenne pepper. Place teriyaki sauce in shallow dish. Dip chicken into teriyaki sauce to coat. Add chicken to flour mixture; shake to coat chicken.

2 Place chicken, bone side down, on large greased baking sheet. Drizzle with melted butter.

3 Bake for about 45 minutes or until chicken is no longer pink (170°F).

Nutrition facts per serving: 293 cal., 9 g total fat (3 g sat. fat), 115 mg chol., 460 mg sodium, 7 g carb., 1 g dietary fiber, 45 g protein.

prosciutto-stuffed
CHICKEN BREASTS WITH PEARS

Prep: 30 minutes
Bake: 45 minutes
Oven: 375°F
Makes: 8 servings

- 8 **bone-in chicken breast halves**
- 1 **5.2-ounce container semisoft cheese with herbs**
- ½ **cup shredded Fontina or mozzarella cheese (2 ounces)**
- ¼ **cup grated Parmesan cheese**
- ¼ **cup chopped prosciutto (about 1½ ounces)**
- 2 **tablespoons butter, melted**
- 1 **tablespoon butter**
- 4 **medium pears, cored and thinly sliced**
- 1 **cup apple juice or apple cider**
- 1 **tablespoon cornstarch**
- 2 **teaspoons snipped fresh sage**

1 Preheat oven to 375°F. Grease a 15x10x1-inch baking pan; set aside.

2 Using your fingers, gently separate the chicken skin from the meat of the breast halves along rib edges, leaving the skin attached along the bone.

3 For stuffing, in a medium bowl, combine cheese with herbs, Fontina cheese, Parmesan cheese, and prosciutto. Spoon cheese mixture under skin of each breast half. Press gently to spread mixture under skin.

4 Place chicken, bone side down, in prepared baking pan. Brush chicken with the 2 tablespoons melted butter. Bake for 45 to 55 minutes or until chicken is no longer pink (170°F).

5 Meanwhile, in a very large skillet, melt the 1 tablespoon butter over medium heat. Add pear slices; cook and stir for 2 to 3 minutes or just until tender. In a small bowl, whisk together apple juice and cornstarch. Add to skillet. Cook and stir until thickened and bubbly. Cook and stir for 2 minutes more. Remove from heat; stir in sage. Serve chicken with pear mixture.

Nutrition facts per serving: 522 cal., 32 g total fat (14 g sat. fat), 152 mg chol., 356 mg sodium, 18 g carb., 3 g dietary fiber, 39 g protein.

creamy WILD RICE–STUFFED CHICKEN BREAST

Prep: 30 minutes
Bake: 35 minutes
Oven: 375°F
Makes: 4 servings

- 2 **tablespoons butter**
- ½ **cup thinly sliced shallots (4)**
- ¼ **cup dry white wine**
- ½ **cup whipping cream**
- 2 **teaspoons snipped fresh thyme**
- 1 **teaspoon salt**
- ½ **teaspoon ground black pepper**
- 1 **cup cooked wild rice**
- ½ **cup shredded smoked Gouda cheese (2 ounces)**
- 3 **tablespoons fine dry bread crumbs**
- 4 **bone-in chicken breast halves**
- 1 **tablespoon butter, melted**

1 Preheat oven to 375°F. Lightly coat a 3-quart rectangular baking dish with cooking spray; set aside. In a medium skillet, melt the 2 tablespoons butter over medium-high heat until bubbly. Add shallots; cook and stir about 3 minutes or just until tender. Remove from heat. Carefully add wine; return to heat. Bring to boiling. Boil gently, uncovered, about 4 minutes or until liquid is almost gone. Stir in cream, thyme, salt, and pepper; boil gently, uncovered, about 5 minutes until slightly thickened. Remove from heat; reserve ⅓ cup. Stir wild rice, cheese, and bread crumbs into remaining cream mixture in skillet.

2 Using your fingers, gently separate chicken skin from breast halves along the rib edges to make a pocket. Spoon one-quarter of the rice mixture under skin of each breast half; press down to create an even layer.

3 Place chicken, bone side down, in prepared dish. Brush with the 1 tablespoon melted butter. Bake for 35 to 40 minutes or until no longer pink (170°F).

4 Transfer chicken to a serving platter. Skim any excess fat from liquid in baking dish; stir in reserved cream mixture, scraping up any drippings from dish. Return to oven for 2 minutes or until heated through. Spoon sauce over chicken.

Nutrition facts per serving: 623 cal., 40 g total fat (20 g sat. fat), 191 mg chol., 1029 mg sodium, 18 g carb., 44 g protein.

oven-barbecued CHICKEN

Use any combination of chicken pieces, whatever is on sale at the supermarket. Bone-in chicken with homemade barbecue sauce is a winning combination.

Prep: 10 minutes
Bake: 45 minutes
Oven: 375°F
Makes: 6 servings

2½ **to 3 pounds meaty chicken pieces (breast halves, thighs, and drumsticks), skinned**

½ **cup chopped onion (1 medium)**

½ **teaspoon bottled minced garlic (1 clove)**

1 **tablespoon cooking oil**

¾ **cup chili sauce**

2 **tablespoons honey**

2 **tablespoons soy sauce**

1 **tablespoon yellow mustard***

½ **teaspoon prepared horseradish**

¼ **teaspoon crushed red pepper**

1 Preheat oven to 375°F. Arrange chicken, bone side up, in an ungreased 15x10x1-inch baking pan. Bake, uncovered, for 25 minutes.

2 Meanwhile, for sauce, in a small saucepan cook onion and garlic in hot oil over medium heat until tender. Stir in chili sauce, honey, soy sauce, mustard, horseradish, and crushed red pepper; heat through.

3 Turn chicken bone side down. Brush chicken with half of the sauce. Bake, uncovered, for 20 to 30 minutes more or until chicken is no longer pink (170°F for breasts, 180°F for thighs and drumsticks). Bring the remaining sauce to a full boil. Pass with chicken.

Nutrition facts per serving: 244 cal., 9 g total fat (2 g sat. fat), 77 mg chol., 807 mg sodium, 15 g carb., 2 g dietary fiber, 26 g protein.

***Tip:** For 1 tablespoon of prepared mustard, use 1 teaspoon dry mustard stirred into 1 tablespoon water.

oven-fried PARMESAN CHICKEN

Prep: 25 minutes
Bake: 45 minutes
Oven: 375°F
Makes: 6 servings

- **1 egg, lightly beaten**
- **2 tablespoons fat-free milk**
- **⅓ cup grated Parmesan cheese**
- **⅓ cup fine dry bread crumbs**
- **1 teaspoon dried oregano, crushed**
- **½ teaspoon paprika**
- **⅛ teaspoon ground black pepper**
- **2½ pounds meaty chicken pieces (breast halves, thighs, and drumsticks), skinned**
- **Nonstick cooking spray**
- **Fresh oregano leaves (optional)**

1 Preheat oven to 375°F. Grease a large shallow baking pan. In a small bowl, combine egg and milk. In a shallow dish, combine Parmesan cheese, bread crumbs, dried oregano, paprika, and pepper.

2 Dip chicken pieces into egg mixture; coat with crumb mixture. Arrange chicken pieces in prepared baking pan, making sure pieces do not touch. Coat tops of chicken pieces with nonstick cooking spray.

3 Bake for 45 to 55 minutes or until chicken is tender and no longer pink (170°F for breasts, 180°F for thighs and drumsticks). Do not turn chicken pieces during baking. If desired, sprinkle with fresh oregano.

Nutrition facts per serving: 219 cal., 9 g total fat (3 g sat. fat), 116 mg chol., 195 mg sodium, 5 g carb., 1 g dietary fiber, 28 g protein.

chicken WITH SPICED TOMATO JAM

Prep: 20 minutes
Bake: 45 minutes
Oven: 350°F
Makes: 6 servings

¾ **cup fine dry bread crumbs**

⅓ **cup grated Romano cheese**

1 **tablespoon snipped fresh chives**

2 **teaspoon chili powder**

¼ **teaspoon salt**

⅛ **teaspoon ground black pepper**

¼ **cup olive oil**

2 **tablespoons Dijon-style mustard**

1 **tablespoons lemon juice**

½ **teaspoon salt**

12 **chicken drumsticks, skinned**

Spiced Tomato Jam*

Snipped fresh chives (optional)

1 Preheat oven to 350°F. Line a baking sheet with parchment paper.

2 Meanwhile, in a shallow dish, combine crumbs, cheese, 1 tablespoon chives, chili powder, ¼ teaspoon salt, and pepper. In a small bowl, combine oil, mustard, lemon juice, and ½ teaspoon salt. Brush chicken with mustard mixture. Roll in crumb mixture to coat. Place on prepared baking sheet.

3 Bake for 45 to 55 minutes or until tender and no longer pink (180°F). Serve with Spiced Tomato Jam. Sprinkle with additional chives.

*Spiced Tomato Jam: In a small saucepan, combine one 14.5-ounce can undrained diced tomatoes, ¼ cup packed brown sugar, 2 tablespoons balsamic vinegar, 2 teaspoons frozen orange juice concentrate, ¼ teaspoon ground cinnamon, ⅛ teaspoon ground ginger, ⅛ teaspoon crushed red pepper, and pinch of ground allspice. Bring to boiling; reduce heat to medium. Simmer, uncovered, for 30 minutes, stirring occasionally until most of liquid has evaporated and jam is thickened. Stir in 1 tablespoon cold butter until melted. Makes about 1 cup.

Nutrition facts per serving: 476 cal., 20 g total fat (5 g sat. fat), 167 mg chol., 905 mg sodium, 25 g carb., 2 g dietary fiber, 46 g protein.

spice-rubbed CHICKEN WITH ROASTED ONIONS

Roasting chickens are larger than broiler-fryer chickens and tend to be juicier. They're ideal for whole-roasting and rotisserie cooking.

Prep: 20 minutes
Roast: 2 hours
Oven: 350°F
Makes: 6 to 8 servings

- **4 cups thickly sliced or quartered red, white, and/or yellow onions and/or boiling or cipollini onions, peeled**
- **¼ teaspoon salt**
- **1 5- to 6-pound whole roasting chicken**
- **1 teaspoon sugar**
- **1 teaspoon garlic powder**
- **1 teaspoon ground cumin**
- **1 teaspoon paprika**
- **1 teaspoon ground coriander**
- **½ teaspoon salt**
- **¼ teaspoon ground cinnamon**
- **¼ teaspoon ground black pepper**
- **⅛ teaspoon ground nutmeg**
- **2 tablespoons olive oil**

1 Preheat oven to 350°F. In a large shallow roasting pan, place half the onions in an even layer. Sprinkle with ¼ teaspoon salt. Fold chicken neck skin onto chicken back, secure with small skewer; tie legs to tail with kitchen string. Tie wings close to body or twist wing tips up and tuck under back of the chicken.

2 In a small bowl, combine sugar and remaining seasonings. Brush chicken all over with oil. Sprinkle on spice mixture and rub in with fingers. Place chicken, breast side up, on onions in pan. If desired, insert meat thermometer into center of inside thigh muscle. (Thermometer should not touch bone.) Loosely cover with foil.

3 Roast for 1 hour. Remove foil. Add remaining onions to pan. Roast, uncovered, for 30 minutes; cut strings on legs and wings. Roast for 30 to 45 minutes more or until drumsticks move easily in their sockets and chicken is no longer pink (180°F in thigh). Cover with foil. Let stand for 15 minutes before carving. Serve chicken with roasted onions.

Nutrition facts per serving: 618 cal., 42 g total fat (11 g sat. fat), 191 mg chol., 438 mg sodium, 9 g carb., 2 g dietary fiber, 49 g protein.

roasted CHICKEN AND SWEET POTATOES

Four different seeds flavor this home-style chicken. When crushed just before adding them to a recipe, cumin seeds and caraway seeds add exciting bursts of flavor.

Prep: 15 minutes
Roast: 1 hour
Stand: 10 minutes
Oven: 375°F
Makes: 6 servings

1 **tablespoon caraway seeds, crushed**

2 **teaspoons dried oregano, crushed**

1 **teaspoon cumin seeds, crushed**

1 **teaspoon ground turmeric**

½ **teaspoon salt**

¼ **teaspoon garlic powder**

⅛ **to ¼ teaspoon ground red pepper**

1 **2½- to 3-pound whole broiler-fryer chicken**

3 **tablespoons olive oil**

4 **medium sweet potatoes, peeled and sliced**

1 **cup apple juice**

1 Preheat oven to 375°F. In a small bowl, combine caraway seeds, oregano, cumin seeds, turmeric, salt, garlic powder, and ground red pepper. Skewer neck skin of chicken to back; tie legs to tail and twist wings under back. Place chicken, breast side up, on a rack in a shallow roasting pan. Brush chicken with 2 tablespoons of the olive oil.

2 Set aside 2 teaspoons of the spice mixture. Rub chicken with remaining spice mixture. Insert a meat thermometer into center of an inside thigh muscle. (Do not allow thermometer bulb to touch bone.) Roast, uncovered, for 20 minutes.

3 Meanwhile, toss sweet potatoes with remaining 1 tablespoon olive oil and the reserved spice mixture. Pour apple juice into roasting pan around chicken. Add potatoes. Continue roasting for 40 to 55 minutes or until meat thermometer registers 180°F to 185°F, drumsticks move easily in their sockets, and potatoes are tender. Remove from oven. Let chicken stand, covered, for 10 minutes before carving. Spoon potatoes into a serving bowl.

Nutrition facts per serving: 346 cal., 17 g total fat (4 g sat. fat), 66 mg chol., 249 mg sodium, 25 g carb., 3 g dietary fiber, 22 g protein.

lemon-rosemary ROAST CHICKEN

The refreshing tang of lemon juice, the bold piney taste of rosemary, and the sharp accent of Dijon-style mustard make this roasted chicken incredibly good.

Prep: 15 minutes
Marinate: 2 to 4 hours
Roast: 25 minutes
Oven: 425°F
Makes: 6 servings

6 **large bone-in chicken breast halves (about 4½ pounds total)**

1 **cup lemon juice**

¼ **cup olive oil**

1 **tablespoon snipped fresh rosemary, or 1 teaspoon dried rosemary, crushed**

2 **tablespoons honey**

2 **tablespoons Dijon-style mustard**

2 **cloves garlic, minced**

¼ **teaspoon salt**

¼ **teaspoon ground black pepper**

1 Place chicken breasts in a resealable plastic bag set in a shallow dish. For marinade, in a small bowl combine lemon juice, oil, rosemary, honey, mustard, garlic, salt, and pepper; mix well. Pour over chicken. Seal bag; turn to coat chicken. Marinate in the refrigerator for 2 to 4 hours, turning bag occasionally.

2 Preheat oven to 425°F. Drain chicken, discarding marinade. Place chicken, bone side down, in a shallow roasting pan. Roast for 25 to 30 minutes or until chicken is golden brown and an instant-read thermometer inserted in the thickest part of a breast registers 170°F.

Nutrition facts per serving: 490 cal., 26 g total fat (7 g sat. fat), 173 mg chol., 195 mg sodium, 3 g carb., 0 g dietary fiber, 57 g protein.

spice-rubbed ROASTED CHICKEN

Prep: 20 minutes
Roast: 1¼ hours
Stand: 10 minutes
Oven: 450°F/350°F
Makes: 6 servings

- 6 **cloves garlic, minced**
- 1 **teaspoon smoked paprika or paprika**
- 1 **teaspoon ground black pepper**
- ½ **teaspoon salt**
- ½ **teaspoon onion powder**
- ½ **teaspoon dried thyme, crushed**
- ¼ **teaspoon dried sage, crushed**
- ¼ **teaspoon cayenne pepper**
- 1 **3½-pound whole roasting chicken**
- 1 **tablespoon olive oil**
  Fresh thyme sprigs (optional)

1 Preheat oven to 450°F. In a small bowl combine garlic, paprika, black pepper, salt, onion powder, dried thyme, sage, and cayenne pepper.

2 Starting at the opening by the leg and thigh, carefully slide your fingertips between the breast and leg meat and the skin to loosen skin from meat. Rub half of the spice mixture between the breast and leg meat and skin. Rub remaining spice mixture on the outside of the chicken. Using 100% cotton kitchen string, tie legs together. Twist wing tips under back.

3 Place chicken, breast side up, on a rack set in a shallow roasting pan. Brush oil on the outside of the chicken. Insert a meat thermometer into center of an inside thigh muscle. (The thermometer should not touch bone.)

4 Roast, uncovered, for 15 minutes. Reduce the oven temperature to 350°F. Continue roasting for about 1 hour more or until drumsticks move easily in their sockets and thermometer registers 180°F (to ensure thighs cook evenly, cut string after 40 minutes of roasting).

5 Remove chicken from oven. Cover chicken with foil and let stand for 10 minutes before carving. If desired, garnish with fresh thyme. While carving, carefully remove and discard the skin of the chicken.

Nutrition facts per serving: 299 cal., 13 g total fat (3 g sat. fat), 127 mg chol., 318 mg sodium, 2 g carb., 0 g dietary fiber, 42 g protein.

roasted CHICKEN WITH FALL VEGETABLES

Prep: 25 minutes
Roast: 1¼ hours
Stand: 10 minutes
Oven: 425°F
Makes: 6 servings

- 6 **cloves garlic, minced**
- 2¾ **teaspoons salt**
- 1½ **teaspoons fresh thyme, or ½ teaspoon dried thyme, crushed**
- ¾ **teaspoon ground black pepper**
- 1 **5½- to 6-pound whole roasting chicken**
- 1 **pound new potatoes, quartered**
- 1 **pound carrots, peeled and cut into 2-inch pieces**
- 1 **pound small white turnips, peeled and cut into 2-inch pieces**
- 1 **pound parsnips, peeled and cut into 2-inch pieces**
- 1 **pound small white onions, peeled**
- 2 **tablespoons vegetable oil**
- ½ **cup dry white wine**
- ¾ **cup chicken broth**

1 Preheat oven to 425°F. Mash garlic with 1 teaspoon of the salt, 1 teaspoon of the fresh thyme (or ¼ teaspoon of the dried thyme), and ½ teaspoon of the pepper to make a paste. Rinse the chicken body cavity; pat dry with paper towels. Rub chicken cavity with 1 teaspoon of the paste. Rub remaining paste under skin of breast.

2 Skewer neck skin of chicken to back; tie legs to tail. Twist wing tips under back. Place chicken, breast side up, on a rack in a shallow roasting pan. If desired, insert a meat thermometer into center of an inside thigh muscle. (The thermometer should not touch bone.) Roast chicken for 15 minutes.

3 Meanwhile, in a stockpot, bring 6 quarts of water and 1 teaspoon of the salt to a boil. Add potatoes, carrots, turnips, parsnips, and onions. Boil for 7 minutes; drain. Return vegetables to pot. Add oil, remaining ½ teaspoon fresh thyme (or ¼ teaspoon dried thyme), remaining ¾ teaspoon salt, and remaining ¼ teaspoon pepper; toss to coat.

4 Arrange vegetables in pan around chicken. Roast for 1 to 1½ hours more or until drumsticks move easily in their sockets and chicken is no longer pink (180°F), stirring vegetables occasionally. Remove from oven. Let stand for 10 minutes before carving chicken.

5 Meanwhile, pour wine and broth into roasting pan. Bring to boiling, stirring to loosen any browned bits from bottom of pan; boil for 2 minutes. Skim off fat. Carve chicken; serve with sauce and vegetables.

Nutrition facts per serving: 740 cal., 36 g total fat (9 g sat. fat), 171 mg chol., 1127 mg sodium, 42 g carb., 59 g protein.

casseroles AND SKILLETS

Potluck Chicken Tetrazzini, *page 180*

potluck CHICKEN TETRAZZINI

The original dish was created in 1908 in San Francisco in honor of opera star Luisa Tetrazzini.

Prep: 30 minutes
Bake: 15 minutes
Cool: 5 minutes
Oven: 350°F
Makes: 10 servings

- 1 **purchased roasted chicken**
- 8 **ounces dried spaghetti or linguine, broken in half**
- 12 **ounces asparagus, trimmed and cut into 1-inch pieces**
- 8 **ounces small whole fresh mushrooms***
- 3 **medium red and/or yellow sweet peppers, seeded and cut into 1-inch pieces**
- 2 **tablespoons butter**
- ¼ **cup all-purpose flour**
- ⅛ **teaspoon ground black pepper**
- 1 **14-ounce can chicken broth**
- ¾ **cup milk**
- ½ **cup shredded Swiss cheese (2 ounces)**
- 1 **tablespoon finely shredded lemon zest**
- 2 **slices sourdough bread, cut into cubes (about 1½ cups)**
- 1 **tablespoon olive oil**
- 2 **tablespoons snipped fresh parsley**

1 Preheat oven to 350°F. Remove meat from chicken; discard bones. Cut chicken pieces in chunks to equal 3 cups. Save remaining chicken for another use.

2 In a Dutch oven, cook spaghetti according to package directions. Add asparagus for the last 1 minute of cooking. Drain. Return to pan.

3 Meanwhile, in a large skillet, cook mushrooms and sweet peppers in hot butter over medium heat for 8 to 10 minutes or until mushrooms are tender, stirring occasionally. Stir in flour and black pepper until well combined. Add broth and milk all at once. Cook and stir until thickened and bubbly.

4 Add mushroom mixture, chicken pieces, Swiss cheese, and half the lemon zest to pasta mixture in Dutch oven. Toss gently to coat. Spoon pasta mixture into 3-quart rectangular baking dish.

5 In a medium bowl, toss together bread cubes, olive oil, and remaining lemon zest. Spread bread cube mixture on pasta mixture. Bake, uncovered, for 15 minutes or until heated through. Let stand for 5 minutes before serving. Sprinkle with parsley before serving.

Nutrition facts per serving: 282 cal., 10 g total fat (4 g sat. fat), 48 mg chol., 258 mg sodium, 28 g carb., 2 g dietary fiber, 20 g protein.

*Tip: If mushrooms are large, cut them in half or in quarters so they are all 1- to 1½-inch pieces.

herbed CHICKEN AND ORZO

Prep: 25 minutes
Bake: 30 minutes
Stand: 5 minutes
Oven: 350°F
Makes: 6 servings

- **8 ounces dried orzo**
- **8 ounces green beans, trimmed and cut into 1-inch pieces (1½ cups)**
- **1 2- to 2¼-pound purchased roasted chicken**
- **2 5.2-ounce containers semisoft cheese with garlic and herbs**
- **½ cup milk**
- **3 medium carrots, shredded (1½ cups)**
- **2 tablespoons snipped fresh flat-leaf parsley**

1 Preheat oven to 350°F. Grease a 3-quart baking dish; set aside.

2 Cook pasta according to package directions, adding green beans for the last 3 minutes of cooking; drain. Meanwhile, cut chicken in 6 pieces.

3 In a large bowl, whisk together cheese and milk until combined. Add cooked pasta mixture; stir gently to coat. Stir in carrots. Transfer mixture to the prepared baking dish. Top with chicken.

4 Bake, covered, for 30 to 40 minutes or until heated through. Let stand for 5 minutes before serving. Sprinkle with parsley.

Nutrition facts per serving: 566 cal., 32 g total fat (16 g sat. fat), 147 mg chol., 685 mg sodium, 37 g carb., 3 g dietary fiber, 31 g protein.

baked CHICKEN CORDON BLEU

Prep: 50 minutes
Bake: 40 minutes
Oven: 350°F
Makes: 6 servings

2   6-ounce packages long grain and wild rice mix
2   cups sliced fresh mushrooms
¼   cup sliced scallions
2   cloves garlic, minced
2   tablespoons butter
2   tablespoons all-purpose flour
2   cups half-and-half or light cream
½   cup shredded Gruyère cheese
2   tablespoons dry sherry (optional)
6   skinless, boneless chicken breast halves (about 2½ pounds total)
3   ounces Gruyère cheese, cut into 3x½x½-inch sticks
6   very thin slices Black Forest ham or country ham
½   teaspoon salt
¼   teaspoon ground black pepper
⅓   cup all-purpose flour
2   eggs, lightly beaten
2   tablespoons water
1½ cups panko (Japanese-style bread crumbs)
¼   cup vegetable oil

1 Preheat oven to 350°F. Prepare rice mixes according to package directions. Spread cooked rice in the bottom of an ungreased 3-quart baking dish.

2 Meanwhile, for sauce, in a medium saucepan cook mushrooms, scallions, and garlic in hot butter over medium heat until tender. Stir in the 2 tablespoons flour. Gradually stir in half-and-half. Cook and stir until thickened and bubbly. Stir in shredded cheese until melted. If desired, stir in sherry. Spoon sauce over rice; cover and keep warm.

3 Starting from the thickest side of each chicken breast half, make a horizontal slit to, but not through, the other side. Wrap each stick of cheese in a slice of ham and insert into a slit. Secure with wooden toothpicks. Sprinkle chicken with salt and pepper.

4 Place the ⅓ cup flour in a shallow dish. In a second shallow dish, combine eggs and water. Place panko in a third shallow dish. Dip chicken in flour, shaking off excess; dip in egg, then in panko, turning to coat.

5 In an extra-large skillet, heat 2 tablespoons of the oil over medium heat. Cook chicken, half at a time, in hot oil for about 4 minutes or until brown on both sides, adding the remaining 2 tablespoons oil with the second batch. Remove toothpicks. Place chicken on top of sauce.

6 Bake, covered, for 40 to 45 minutes or until chicken is no longer pink (170°F).

Nutrition facts per serving: 862 cal., 36 g total fat (15 g sat. fat), 256 mg chol., 1586 mg sodium, 66 g carb., 3 g dietary fiber, 68 g protein.

cajun CHICKEN PASTA

This rich, creamy dish is ideal for time-pressed cooks. It can be assembled up to 24 hours before baking, so you can arrive at the party—hot dish in hand—as cool as a cucumber.

Prep: 50 minutes
Bake: 25 minutes
Oven: 350°F
Makes: 8 to 10 servings

1 **pound bow-tie or rotini pasta**

4 **skinless, boneless chicken breast halves (about 1¼ pounds total)**

2 **tablespoons all-purpose flour**

2 **tablespoons salt-free Cajun seasoning**

1 **tablespoon vegetable oil**

2 **cups heavy cream**

2 **cups shredded cheddar and Monterey Jack cheese blend (8 ounces)**

½ **teaspoon salt**

3 **cups seeded, diced tomatoes (3 large)**

¼ **cup sliced scallions (2)**

Hot pepper sauce, for serving (optional)

1 Preheat oven to 350°F. Cook pasta according to package directions. Drain well; return pasta to pan.

2 Cut chicken into 1-inch pieces. In a large food-storage bag, place chicken pieces, flour, and 1 tablespoon of the Cajun seasoning; seal and toss to coat. Heat oil in a large skillet over medium-high heat. Add chicken; cook and stir until chicken is no longer pink. Set chicken aside.

3 In a medium saucepan, bring cream just to a boil over medium heat, stirring occasionally. Remove from heat; whisk in 1 cup of the cheese, the remaining 1 tablespoon Cajun seasoning, and the salt until cheese is melted and mixture is smooth.

4 In a very large bowl, combine cooked pasta, cooked chicken, cream mixture, tomatoes, and the remaining 1 cup cheese. Transfer mixture to greased 13x9x2-inch baking dish.

5 Bake, covered, for 25 to 30 minutes or until mixture is heated through. Sprinkle with scallions before serving. If desired, pass hot pepper sauce at the table.

Nutrition facts per serving: 641 cal., 35 g total fat (20 g sat. fat), 151 mg chol., 448 mg sodium, 49 g carb., 3 g dietary fiber, 33 g protein.

Make-Ahead Directions: Prepare casserole as directed through Step 4. Cover with plastic wrap, then foil, and refrigerate for up to 24 hours. To serve, preheat oven to 350°F. Remove plastic wrap. Bake casserole, covered with foil, for 35 to 40 minutes or until mixture is heated through.

chicken AND BROCCOLI CASSEROLE

Prep: 10 minutes
Cook: 4 hours (low) or
3 hours (high)
Makes: 4 servings

- **1 cup shredded cheddar cheese**
- **1 tablespoon cornstarch**
- **1 pound boneless, skinless chicken breast, cut into 1-inch pieces**
- **1 10-ounce package frozen chopped broccoli**
- **1 medium onion, chopped**
- **½ cup low-sodium chicken broth**
- **½ teaspoon salt**
- **½ teaspoon ground black pepper**
- **4 tablespoons crushed cheddar cheese crackers (optional)**
- **3 cups cooked white or brown rice (optional)**

1 Toss together ½ cup of the cheddar cheese and the cornstarch.

2 Place chicken, broccoli, onion, broth, ¼ teaspoon each salt and pepper, and the cheddar-cornstarch mixture into slow cooker. Cover and cook on low-heat setting for 4 hours or on high-heat setting for 3 hours.

3 Remove lid and stir remaining ½ cup cheddar cheese and ¼ teaspoon each salt and pepper into slow cooker. Sprinkle crushed crackers over top and serve immediately with rice, if desired.

Nutrition facts per serving: 286 cal., 11 g total fat (6 g sat. fat), 96 mg chol., 633 mg sodium, 9 g carb., 2 g dietary fiber, 35 g protein.

dutch CHICKEN DELIGHT

Besides wooden shoes, the Dutch are famed for exceptionally rich and especially homey cuisine. This yummy recipe is a perfect example.

Prep: 30 minutes
Bake: 40 minutes
Oven: 350°F
Makes: 6 to 8 servings

- 12 **ounces dried egg noodles**
- 3 **slices bacon, halved crosswise**
- 1½ **pounds skinless, boneless chicken breast halves, cut into 1-inch pieces**
- 1 **10.75-ounce can condensed cream of mushroom soup**
- 1¼ **cups milk**
- 1 **8-ounce carton sour cream**
- ½ **of a 4.5-ounce jar sliced dried beef, coarsely chopped (about ¾ cup)**
- **Celery leaves**

1 Preheat oven to 350°F. Cook noodles according to package directions; drain. Spoon noodles into a 13x9-inch baking dish.

2 Meanwhile, in a large skillet, cook bacon on medium heat until crisp. Drain on paper towels, reserving drippings in skillet. Cook and stir chicken, half at a time, in the reserved drippings for about 4 minutes or until no longer pink. Drain off fat.

3 In a medium bowl, combine cream of mushroom soup, milk, and sour cream. Add cooked chicken, soup mixture, and dried beef to cooked noodles in dish; stir gently to combine.

4 Cover with foil. Bake for about 40 minutes or until heated through, stirring once halfway through baking. Top with bacon and sprinkle with celery leaves.

Nutrition facts per serving: 588 cal., 25 g total fat (10 g sat. fat), 158 mg chol., 920 mg sodium, 48 g carb., 2 g dietary fiber, 43 g protein.

chicken AND STUFFING CASSEROLE

If you're going to take a dish to a gathering with people you don't know, don't worry. A casserole of chicken and stuffing always satisfies!

Prep: 25 minutes
Cook: 4½ to 5 hours (low)
Makes: 16 to 20 servings

½ cup **butter or margarine**

1 cup **thinly sliced celery (2 stalks)**

¾ cup **chopped onions (2 small)**

1 **6-ounce package long grain and wild rice mix**

1 **14-ounce package herb-seasoned stuffing croutons**

4 cups **cubed cooked chicken (20 ounces)**

1 **4.5-ounce jar (drained weight) sliced mushrooms, drained**

¼ cup **snipped fresh parsley**

1½ teaspoons **poultry seasoning**

¼ teaspoon **ground black pepper**

2 **eggs, lightly beaten**

2 **14-ounce cans reduced-sodium chicken broth**

1 **10.75-ounce can reduced-fat and reduced-sodium condensed cream of chicken or cream of mushroom soup**

1 In a large skillet, heat butter over medium heat. Add celery and onions; cook for about 5 minutes or until vegetables are tender.

2 Lightly coat the inside of a 5½- or 6-quart slow cooker with nonstick cooking spray. Add uncooked rice from mix (reserve seasoning packet until needed). Using a slotted spoon, transfer celery and onion to cooker, reserving butter. Stir to combine.

3 Place croutons in a very large bowl. Stir in the reserved butter, the chicken, drained mushrooms, parsley, poultry seasoning, pepper, and the contents of the seasoning packet from rice mix.

4 In a medium bowl, combine eggs, broth, and soup. Pour over crouton mixture, tossing gently to combine. Transfer mixture to cooker.

5 Cover and cook on low-heat setting (do not use high-heat setting) for 4½ to 5 hours. Stir gently before serving.

Nutrition facts per serving: 287 cal., 11 g total fat (5 g sat. fat), 76 mg chol., 903 mg sodium, 31 g carb., 3 g dietary fiber, 16 g protein.

chicken ENCHILADAS

Prep: 30 minutes
Bake: 40 minutes
Oven: 350°F
Makes: 6 servings

¼ **cup slivered almonds, toasted**

¼ **cup chopped onion**

1 **to 2 medium fresh jalapeño chile peppers, seeded and chopped* (optional)**

2 **tablespoons butter or margarine**

1 **4-ounce can diced green chile peppers, drained**

1 **3-ounce package cream cheese, softened**

1 **tablespoon milk**

1 **teaspoon ground cumin**

3 **cups chopped cooked chicken**

12 **7-inch flour tortillas or 6-inch corn tortillas**

1 **10.75-ounce can condensed cream of chicken or cream of mushroom soup**

1 **8-ounce carton sour cream**

1 **cup milk**

¾ **cup shredded Monterey Jack or cheddar cheese (3 ounces)**

2 **tablespoons slivered almonds, toasted**

1 Preheat oven to 350°F. Grease a 3-quart rectangular baking dish. In a medium skillet, cook the ¼ cup almonds, the onion, and the jalapeño peppers (if using) in hot butter over medium heat until onion is tender. Remove skillet from heat. Stir in 1 tablespoon of the canned chile peppers; reserve remaining peppers for sauce.

2 In a medium bowl, combine cream cheese, the 1 tablespoon milk, and cumin; add nut mixture and chicken. Stir until combined. Spoon about ¼ cup of the chicken mixture onto each tortilla near an edge; roll up. Place filled tortillas, seam side down, in prepared baking dish.

3 For sauce, in a medium bowl combine soup, sour cream, 1 cup milk, and reserved chile peppers. Pour evenly over the tortillas in baking dish. Cover with foil.

4 Bake for about 35 minutes or until heated through. Remove foil. Sprinkle enchiladas with cheese and the 2 tablespoons almonds. Return to oven; bake for about 5 minutes more or until cheese melts.

Nutrition facts per serving: 660 cal., 38 g total fat (16 g sat. fat), 127 mg chol., 1140 mg sodium, 44 g carb., 3 g dietary fiber, 35 g protein.

*Tip: Because chile peppers contain volatile oils that can burn your skin and eyes, avoid direct contact with them as much as possible. When working with chile peppers, wear plastic or rubber gloves. If your bare hands do touch the peppers, wash your hands and nails well with soap and warm water.

chicken CHOW MEIN CASEROLE

Prep: 25 minutes
Bake: 50 minutes
Oven: 350°F
Makes: 8 servings

4 cups chopped cooked
   chicken

4 stalks celery, chopped
   (2 cups)

2 medium carrots, shredded
   (1 cup)

1 cup chopped red sweet
   pepper

2 4-ounce cans (drained
   weight) sliced
   mushrooms, drained

⅔ cup sliced or slivered
   almonds, toasted

2 tablespoons diced
   pimiento, drained

2 10.75-ounce cans
   condensed cream of
   chicken soup

2 cups chow mein noodles

1 Preheat oven to 350°F. In an extra-large bowl, stir together chicken, celery, carrots, sweet pepper, mushrooms, almonds, and pimiento. Add soup to chicken mixture; mix well.

2 Transfer chicken mixture to an ungreased 3-quart rectangular baking dish. Bake, covered, for 45 minutes. Sprinkle with chow mein noodles. Bake, uncovered, for 5 to 10 minutes more or until heated through.

Nutrition facts per serving: 366 cal., 19 g total fat (4 g sat. fat), 68 mg chol., 921 mg sodium, 21 g carb., 4 g dietary fiber, 27 g protein.

chicken ALFREDO POT PIES

Prep: 25 minutes
Bake: 12 minutes
Oven: 450°F
Makes: 4 servings

½ **of a 15-ounce package (1 crust) rolled refrigerated unbaked piecrust***

3 **cups frozen vegetable blend (any combination)**

3 **cups cubed cooked chicken or turkey**

1 **10-ounce container refrigerated Alfredo pasta sauce**

1 **teaspoon dried thyme, marjoram, or sage, crushed**

Fresh thyme or marjoram sprigs (optional)

1 Let piecrust stand according to package directions. Preheat oven to 450°F. In a large skillet, cook frozen vegetables in a small amount of boiling water for 5 minutes; drain. Return to skillet. Stir in chicken, Alfredo sauce, and the dried thyme. Cook and stir until bubbly. Divide mixture among 4 ungreased 10-ounce individual casseroles or custard cups.

2 On a lightly floured surface, roll piecrust into a 13-inch circle. Cut four 5-inch circles and place on top of casseroles. Press edges of pastry firmly against sides of casseroles. Cut slits in tops for steam to escape.*

3 Place casseroles in a foil-lined shallow baking pan. Bake, uncovered, for 12 to 15 minutes or until mixture is heated through and pastry is golden. If desired, garnish with fresh thyme.

Nutrition facts per serving: 709 cal., 41 g total fat (19 g sat. fat), 143 mg chol., 596 mg sodium, 45 g carb., 4 g dietary fiber, 38 g protein.

***Tip:** Instead of cutting slits for steam to escape, use a small cookie cutter to cut shapes from pastry. Brush pastry with a little milk or water and top with pastry cutouts.

hot CHICKEN SALAD

A crunchy cornflake-almond topper complements the saucy chicken mixture.

Prep: 20 minutes
Bake: 30 minutes
Stand: 10 minutes
Oven: 400°F
Makes: 6 servings

3 cups cubed cooked chicken breast (about 1 pound)

1 cup sliced celery

1 cup chopped yellow or red sweet pepper

¾ cup shredded reduced-fat cheddar or mozzarella cheese (3 ounces)

1 10.75-ounce can reduced-fat and reduced-sodium condensed cream of chicken soup

1 6-ounce carton low-fat plain yogurt

¼ cup sliced scallions

1 tablespoon lemon juice

¼ teaspoon ground black pepper

½ cup crushed cornflakes

¼ cup sliced almonds

1 Preheat oven to 400°F. In a large bowl, stir together chicken, celery, sweet pepper, cheese, soup, yogurt, scallions, lemon juice, and black pepper. Transfer to a 2-quart rectangular baking dish.

2 In a small bowl, stir together cornflakes and almonds. Sprinkle evenly over chicken mixture.

3 Bake, uncovered, for about 30 minutes or until heated through. Let stand for 10 minutes before serving.

Nutrition facts per serving: 251 cal., 9 g total fat (4 g sat. fat), 75 mg chol., 415 mg sodium, 13 g carb., 2 g dietary fiber, 29 g protein.

chicken AND WILD RICE CASSEROLE

Prep: 30 minutes
Bake: 35 minutes
Oven: 350°F
Makes: 4 servings

1 **6-ounce package long
    grain and wild rice mix**

1 **medium onion, chopped
    (½ cup)**

1 **stalk celery, chopped
    (½ cup)**

2 **tablespoons butter**

1 **10.5- or 10.75-ounce can
    condensed chicken with
    white and wild rice soup
    or cream of chicken soup**

½ **cup sour cream**

⅓ **cup dry white wine or
    chicken broth**

2 **tablespoons snipped
    fresh basil, or ½ teaspoon
    dried basil, crushed**

2 **cups shredded cooked
    chicken or turkey**

⅓ **cup finely shredded
    Parmesan cheese**

1 Prepare rice mix according to package directions.

2 Meanwhile, preheat oven to 350°F. In a large skillet, cook onion and celery in hot butter over medium heat until tender. Stir in soup, sour cream, wine, and basil. Stir in cooked rice and chicken.

3 Transfer mixture to an ungreased 2-quart baking dish. Sprinkle with cheese. Bake, uncovered, for about 35 minutes or until heated through.

Nutrition facts per serving: 468 cal., 19 g total fat (9 g sat. fat), 98 mg chol., 1339 mg sodium, 43 g carb., 3 g dietary fiber, 29 g protein.

pizza CASSEROLE

Several favorite pizza ingredients get tucked under a lattice topping easily made from refrigerated breadsticks.

Prep: 10 minutes
Cook: 17 minutes
Bake: 25 minutes
Oven: 350°F
Makes: 8 servings

1 tablespoon extra-virgin olive oil

1 medium onion, chopped

2 sweet yellow, red, or green peppers, seeded and cut into large dice

2 medium zucchini, cut into rounds

2 cloves garlic, chopped

3 14.5-ounce cans no-salt-added diced tomatoes, drained

5 cooked chicken sausages (about 12 ounces total), sliced

1 teaspoon dried Italian seasoning*

1 teaspoon salt

½ teaspoon ground black pepper

¼ cup grated Parmesan cheese

2 cups shredded mozzarella cheese (8 ounces)

1 tube (11 ounces) refrigerated breadsticks

1 Preheat oven to 350°F. Grease 13x9x2-inch baking dish. In a large skillet, heat oil over medium-high heat. Add onion and sweet peppers; cook for 5 minutes. Add zucchini and garlic; cook for about 5 minutes or until barely tender.

2 Add tomatoes, sausage, Italian seasoning, salt, and black pepper; cook for 5 to 7 minutes or until somewhat dry. Add 2 tablespoons Parmesan cheese. Spoon half of the tomato mixture into prepared dish. Top with 1 cup mozzarella cheese. Add remaining tomato mixture. Arrange breadsticks on top in lattice pattern, trimming to fit. Sprinkle with the remaining 2 tablespoons Parmesan cheese and the remaining 1 cup mozzarella cheese.

3 Bake for about 25 minutes or until breadsticks are browned and filling is bubbly.

Nutrition facts per serving: 321 cal., 14 g total fat (6 g sat. fat), 73 mg chol., 988 mg sodium, 30 g carb., 4 g dietary fiber, 19 g protein.

*Tip: Dried Italian seasoning is typically a mixture of basil, oregano, thyme, and rosemary (with garlic and red pepper sometimes added). If you happen to be out of the seasoning blend, substitute a combination of herbs typically used in the mixture.

ginger CHICKEN AND WARM APPLE SLAW

Start to Finish: 15 minutes
Makes: 4 servings

- **4 skinless, boneless chicken breast halves (1¼ to 1½ pounds total)**
- **½ teaspoon salt**
- **¼ teaspoon ground black pepper**
- **1 tablespoon olive oil**
- **1 red onion, cut into thin wedges**
- **1 tablespoon grated fresh ginger**
- **½ cup chicken broth**
- **2 tablespoons cider vinegar**
- **2 red and/or green cooking apples, cored and cut into ¼-inch strips**
- **3 cups packaged shredded cabbage with carrot (coleslaw mix)**
- **Orange wedges**

1 Season chicken with salt and pepper. In a large skillet, cook chicken in hot oil over medium-high heat for 4 minutes. Turn chicken and add onion and ginger. Cook for 4 to 5 minutes more, stirring onions, until chicken is no longer pink (170°F). Transfer chicken to a platter; keep warm.

2 Add broth and vinegar to skillet. Bring to boiling; boil gently, uncovered, for 5 minutes or until reduced by about half. Add apples and coleslaw mix. Cook and stir gently for about 5 minutes or until apples and cabbage are just tender. Return chicken and any accumulated juices to skillet. Serve with orange wedges for squeezing over top.

Nutrition facts per serving: 270 cal., 5 g fat, (1 g sat. fat), 83 mg chol., 518 mg sodium, 20 g carb., 4 g dietary fiber, 34 g protein.

chicken PARMIGIANA

Prep: 30 minutes
Cook: 25 minutes
Makes: 4 servings

⅓ **cup chopped onion**

1 **clove garlic, minced**

1 **tablespoon butter or margarine**

1 **14.5-ounce can diced tomatoes, undrained**

½ **teaspoon sugar**

⅛ **teaspoon salt**

Pinch of ground black pepper

¼ **cup snipped fresh basil**

4 **skinless, boneless chicken breast halves (1 to 1¼ pounds total)**

⅓ **cup seasoned fine dry bread crumbs**

3 **tablespoons grated Parmesan cheese**

½ **teaspoon dried oregano, crushed**

1 **egg, beaten**

2 **tablespoons milk**

3 **tablespoons olive oil or cooking oil**

¼ **cup shredded mozzarella cheese (1 ounce)**

1 **tablespoon grated Parmesan cheese**

1 For sauce, in a medium saucepan cook onion and garlic in hot butter until onion is tender. Carefully stir in tomatoes, sugar, salt, and pepper. Bring to boiling; reduce heat. Simmer, uncovered, for 10 minutes or to desired consistency, stirring occasionally. Stir in basil. Keep warm.

2 Meanwhile, with a meat mallet, pound each chicken breast half between pieces of plastic wrap to a ¼-inch thickness.

3 In a shallow dish, stir together bread crumbs, the 3 tablespoons Parmesan cheese, and oregano. In another bowl, stir together the egg and milk. Dip chicken breast halves in egg mixture, then in crumb mixture to coat. In a 12-inch skillet, cook chicken in hot oil over medium heat for 2 to 3 minutes on each side or until golden. Transfer chicken to a serving platter.

4 Spoon sauce over chicken. Top with shredded mozzarella and 1 tablespoon Parmesan cheese. Let stand for about 2 minutes or until cheese melts.

Nutrition facts per 3 ounces chicken or veal + ⅓ cup sauce: 379 cal., 20 g total fat (6 g sat. fat), 137 mg chol., 711 mg sodium, 15 g carb., 1 g dietary fiber, 34 g protein.

Creamy Tomato Chicken Parmigiana: Prepare as above, except after simmering the sauce for 10 minutes or to desired consistency, slowly add 3 tablespoons whipping cream, half-and-half, or light cream, stirring constantly. Cook and stir for 3 minutes more and then stir in the basil.

Nutrition Facts per 3 ounces cooked chicken plus ⅓ cup sauce: 418 cal., 24 g total fat (9 g sat. fat), 152 mg chol., 715 mg sodium, 15 g carb., 1 g dietary fiber, 34 g protein.

chicken AND BROCCOLI STIR-FRY

Start to Finish: 30 minutes
Makes: 4 servings

½ **cup water**

2 **tablespoons soy sauce**

2 **tablespoons hoisin sauce**

2 **teaspoons cornstarch**

1 **teaspoon grated fresh ginger**

1 **teaspoon toasted sesame oil**

1 **pound broccoli**

1 **yellow sweet pepper**

2 **tablespoons cooking oil**

12 **ounces skinless, boneless chicken breast halves, cut into bite-size pieces**

2 **cups chow mein noodles**

   Toasted sesame seeds (optional)

   Hoisin sauce (optional)

1 For sauce, in a small bowl stir together the water, soy sauce, hoisin sauce, cornstarch, ginger, and sesame oil, set aside.

2 Cut florets from broccoli stems and separate florets into small pieces. Cut broccoli stems crosswise into ¼-inch-thick slices. Cut sweet pepper into short, thin strips.

3 In a wok or large skillet, heat 1 tablespoon of the cooking oil over medium-high heat. Cook and stir broccoli stems in hot oil for 1 minute. Add broccoli florets and sweet pepper; cook and stir for 3 to 4 minutes or until crisp-tender. Remove from wok.

4 Add remaining 1 tablespoon oil to wok. Add chicken; cook and stir for 2 to 3 minutes or until no longer pink. Push chicken from center of wok. Stir sauce; pour into center of wok. Cook and stir until thickened and bubbly. Return cooked vegetables to wok. Stir together to coat. Cook and stir for 1 minute or until heated through. Serve over chow mein noodles. If desired, garnish with toasted sesame seeds and serve with additional hoisin sauce.

Nutrition facts per serving: 378 cal., 16 g total fat (3 g sat. fat), 49 mg chol., 877 mg sodium, 31 g carb., 6 g dietary fiber, 29 g protein.

mango-chili CHICKEN STIR-FRY

Start to Finish: 25 minutes
Makes: 4 servings

⅓ **cup bottled mango chutney, snipped**

2 **teaspoons Asian chili-garlic sauce**

1 **teaspoon minced fresh ginger**

2 **cloves garlic, minced**

2 **teaspoons cooking oil**

1 **to 3 small dried hot chile peppers***

1 **pound skinless, boneless chicken breast halves, cut into ¾- to 1-inch pieces**

1 **red sweet pepper, cut into 1- to 2-inch strips**

2 **cups hot cooked rice**

1 **mango, peeled, pitted, and cut into thin strips**

For sauce, in a small bowl combine chutney, chili-garlic sauce, ginger, and garlic. In a large wok or very large nonstick skillet, heat oil over medium-high heat. Add chile peppers; cook and stir for 10 seconds.** Add chicken; cook and stir for 3 to 4 minutes or until no longer pink. Push chicken to edges of pan. Add sweet pepper strips. Cook and stir for 1 minute. Add sauce, stirring to coat all, and heat through. Serve over rice and top with mango strips.

Nutrition facts per serving: 367 cal., 5 g total fat (1 g sat. fat), 66 mg chol., 124 mg sodium, 52 g carb., 3 g dietary fiber, 29 g protein.

***Tip:** Because chile peppers contain volatile oils that can burn your skin and eyes, avoid direct contact with them as much as possible. When working with chile peppers, wear plastic or rubber gloves. If your bare hands do touch the peppers, wash your hands and nails well with soap and warm water.

****Tip:** Be sure the area is well ventilated when cooking the hot peppers.

chicken CURRY SKILLET WITH RICE NOODLES

Start to Finish: 30 minutes
Makes: 6 servings

- **8 ounces wide rice noodles, broken**
- **1½ pounds skinless, boneless chicken breast halves, cut into 1-inch pieces**
- **2 tablespoons vegetable oil**
- **1 16-ounce package frozen green bean or sugar snap pea stir-fry vegetables, thawed**
- **1 14-ounce can unsweetened light coconut milk**
- **½ cup water**
- **1 tablespoon sugar**
- **1 tablespoon fish sauce**
- **½ to 1 teaspoon red curry paste**
- **¼ teaspoon salt**
- **¼ teaspoon ground black pepper**
- **¼ cup snipped fresh basil**

1 Soak rice noodles according to package directions; drain.

2 In a 12-inch skillet, cook chicken in hot oil over medium heat for 8 to 10 minutes or until chicken is longer pink, adding stir-fry vegetables for the last 4 minutes of cooking. Remove chicken mixture from skillet.

3 In the same skillet, combine coconut milk, water, sugar, fish sauce, curry paste, salt, and black pepper. Bring to boiling. Stir in rice noodles and chicken mixture. Return to boiling; reduce heat. Simmer, uncovered, for about 2 minutes or until noodles are tender but still firm and sauce is thickened. Sprinkle with basil.

Nutrition facts per serving: 386 cal., 10 g total fat (3 g sat. fat), 66 mg chol., 529 mg sodium, 42 g carb., 2 g dietary fiber, 28 g protein.

chicken PICCATA

Start to Finish: 20 minutes
Makes: 4 servings

- **4 skinless, boneless chicken breast halves (1¼ to 1½ pounds total)**
- **1 tablespoon Dijon-style mustard**
- **Salt and ground black pepper**
- **¼ cup seasoned fine dry bread crumbs**
- **¼ cup olive oil**
- **8 ounces green beans, trimmed**
- **2 lemons, 1 sliced and 1 juiced**
- **1 tablespoon capers**

1 Place each chicken breast half between pieces of plastic wrap. Using the flat side of a meat mallet, pound chicken lightly to about ¼ inch thick. Remove plastic wrap. Brush chicken with mustard; sprinkle evenly with salt, pepper, and bread crumbs to coat.

2 In a large skillet, cook chicken in 2 tablespoons hot oil over medium-high heat for 6 to 8 minutes or until no longer pink, turning once. Transfer chicken to serving plates.

3 Add remaining 2 tablespoons oil to the skillet. Add green beans; cook over medium heat for about 4 minutes or until crisp-tender, stirring occasionally. Add lemon slices for the last minute of cooking. Divide beans and lemon slices among plates. Add lemon juice and capers to skillet; heat through. Drizzle over chicken.

Nutrition facts per serving: 362 cal., 16 g total fat (3 g sat. fat), 99 mg chol., 546 mg sodium, 13 g carb., 4 g dietary fiber, 42 g protein.

smoky CHICKEN SUCCOTASH SKILLET

Prep: 20 minutes
Cook: 15 minutes
Makes: 4 to 6 servings

1   **16-ounce package frozen whole kernel corn**

1   **12-ounce package edamame (frozen sweet soybeans) or one 16-ounce package frozen baby lima beans**

1¾ **cups water**

    Finely shredded zest and juice of 1 lime

1   **2-pound deli-roasted chicken, cut into 6 to 8 pieces**

1   **16-ounce jar chipotle salsa**

    Lime wedges (optional)

In a very large skillet, combine corn and edamame; add water. Bring to boiling; reduce heat. Simmer, uncovered, for 5 to 6 minutes or until edamame are just tender. Add lime zest and lime juice to skillet. Stir until combined. Place chicken pieces atop corn mixture. Pour salsa over all. Cook, covered, over medium heat for 10 minutes or until heated through. If desired, serve with lime wedges.

Nutrition facts per serving: 621 cal., 28 g total fat (7 g sat. fat), 134 mg chol., 823 mg sodium, 41 g carb., 8 g dietary fiber, 58 g protein.

grilled

Thai Thighs, *page 210*

thai THIGHS

When handling red curry paste, it's important to remember that it contains seeded peppers and other volatile oils. Wash hands thoroughly and avoid contact with skin and eyes.

Prep: 30 minutes
Marinate: 8 to 24 hours
Grill: 50 minutes
Makes: 6 servings

- 12 **chicken thighs (4½ to 5 pounds total), skinned (if desired)**
- ⅔ **cup snipped fresh basil**
- ⅔ **cup snipped fresh cilantro**
- 2 **tablespoons packed brown sugar**
- 12 **cloves garlic, minced**
- 2 **tablespoons grated fresh ginger**
- 2 **tablespoons soy sauce**
- 1 **tablespoon fish sauce**
- 1 **tablespoon toasted sesame oil**
- 2 **teaspoons red curry paste**
- ½ **cup honey-roasted peanuts, chopped**

1 Place chicken in a resealable plastic bag set in a large bowl. For marinade, in a small bowl combine ⅓ cup of the basil, ⅓ cup of the cilantro, the brown sugar, garlic, ginger, soy sauce, fish sauce, oil, and curry paste. Rub marinade over chicken. Seal bag; turn to coat chicken. Marinate in the refrigerator for 8 to 24 hours, turning bag occasionally. Drain chicken, scraping off and discarding marinade.

2 For a charcoal grill, arrange medium-hot coals around a drip pan. Test for medium heat above pan. Place chicken, meaty side down, on grill rack over drip pan. Cover and grill for 50 to 60 minutes or until chicken is no longer pink (180°F), turning once halfway through grilling. (For a gas grill, preheat grill. Reduce heat to medium. Adjust for indirect cooking. Grill as above.)

3 Meanwhile, in a small bowl, combine the remaining ⅓ cup basil, the remaining ⅓ cup cilantro, and peanuts. Sprinkle chicken with basil mixture.

Nutrition facts per serving: 653 cal., 45 g total fat (12 g sat. fat), 224 mg chol., 865 mg sodium, 10 g carb., 1 g dietary fiber, 49 g protein.

tequila-marinated
CHICKEN THIGHS

Chicken thighs are more flavorful than white meat, so they need little assistance. The margarita-inspired marinade in this recipe adds the perfect amount of flavor.

Prep: 15 minutes
Marinate: 4 to 6 hours
Grill: 50 minutes
Makes: 6 servings

12 **chicken thighs (4½ to 5 pounds total), skinned (if desired)**

½ **cup orange juice**

¼ **cup tequila**

2 **tablespoons lime juice**

1 **tablespoon finely chopped canned chipotle chile pepper in adobo sauce**

1 **teaspoon snipped fresh oregano**

2 **cloves garlic, minced**

½ **teaspoon salt**

¼ **teaspoon ground black pepper**

1 Place chicken in a resealable plastic bag set in a large bowl. For marinade, in a small bowl combine orange juice, tequila, lime juice, chipotle pepper, oregano, garlic, salt, and black pepper. Pour marinade over chicken. Seal bag; turn to coat chicken. Marinate in the refrigerator for 4 to 6 hours, turning bag occasionally. Drain chicken, reserving marinade.

2 For a charcoal grill, arrange medium-hot coals around a drip pan. Test for medium heat above pan. Place chicken, meaty side down, on grill rack over drip pan. Cover and grill for 50 to 60 minutes or until chicken is no longer pink (180°F), turning and brushing once with reserved marinade halfway through grilling. (For a gas grill, preheat grill. Reduce heat to medium. Adjust for indirect cooking. Grill as above.) Discard any remaining marinade.

Nutrition facts per serving: 432 cal., 29 g total fat (8 g sat. fat), 158 mg chol., 349 mg sodium, 3 g carb., 0 g dietary fiber, 33 g protein.

all-american BARBECUED CHICKEN

Prep: 30 minutes
Marinate: 4 to 6 hours
Grill: 50 minutes
Makes: 4 to 6 servings

3 to 3½ pounds meaty chicken pieces (breast halves, thighs, and drumsticks)
3 tablespoons lemon juice
1 tablespoon vegetable oil
1 teaspoon salt
½ teaspoon ground black pepper
1 clove garlic, minced
1 cup Balsamic BBQ Sauce*

1 Place chicken in a large resealable plastic bag set in a shallow dish. For marinade, stir together lemon juice, oil, salt, pepper, and garlic. Pour over chicken; seal bag. Marinate in the refrigerator for 4 to 6 hours, turning bag occasionally.

2 Drain chicken, discarding marinade. For a charcoal grill, arrange medium-hot coals around a drip pan. Test for medium heat above the pan. Place chicken, bone side down, on grill rack over drip pan. Cover and grill for 50 to 60 minutes or until chicken is no longer pink (170°F for breast halves, 180°F for thighs and drumsticks), brushing with half of the Balsamic BBQ Sauce during the last 15 minutes of grilling. (For a gas grill, preheat grill. Reduce heat to medium. Adjust for indirect cooking. Place chicken pieces on grill rack over burner that is off. Grill as above.)

3 To serve, pass the remaining Balsamic BBQ Sauce with the chicken.

*Balsamic BBQ Sauce: In a medium saucepan, combine 1 cup lager beer, 1 cup ketchup, ½ cup packed brown sugar, ⅓ cup white balsamic vinegar, 6 cloves minced garlic, 1 tablespoon honey, 1 teaspoon ground cumin, 1 teaspoon Asian chile sauce (if desired), 1 teaspoon chili powder, and ½ teaspoon ground black pepper. Bring to boiling; reduce heat. Simmer, uncovered, for 45 minutes to 1 hour or until mixture reaches desired consistency, stirring frequently. (Cover and chill any leftovers for up to 1 week. Before serving, warm sauce in saucepan.)

Nutrition facts per serving: 630 cal., 37 g total fat (10 g sat. fat), 173 mg chol., 900 mg sodium, 26 g carb., 1 g dietary fiber, 44 g protein.

tandoori SPICED CHICKEN

Prep: 20 minutes
Marinate: 2 to 4 hours
Grill: 50 minutes
Makes: 6 servings

3 **cups buttermilk**

¼ **cup coarse kosher salt**

2 **tablespoons sugar**

4 **cloves garlic, minced**

1 **tablespoon ground ginger**

1 **tablespoon curry powder**

1½ **teaspoons onion powder**

¾ **teaspoon cayenne pepper**

2½ **to 3 pounds meaty chicken pieces (breast halves, thighs, and drumsticks), skinned**

Curry-Cucumber Sauce*

1 For brine, in a large bowl combine buttermilk, salt, sugar, and garlic. In a small bowl, combine ginger, curry powder, onion powder, and cayenne pepper; reserve 2 teaspoons of the ginger mixture. Stir remaining ginger mixture into buttermilk mixture; stir to dissolve salt and sugar. Place chicken in a large resealable plastic bag set in a shallow dish. Pour buttermilk mixture over chicken; seal bag. Marinate in the refrigerator for at least 2 hours or up to 4 hours, turning bag occasionally.

2 Drain and discard marinade. Sprinkle chicken evenly with reserved ginger mixture.

3 For a charcoal grill, arrange medium-hot coals around a drip pan. Test for medium heat above the pan. Place chicken, bone side down, on grill rack over drip pan. Cover and grill for 50 to 60 minutes or until chicken is no longer pink (170°F for breast halves, 180°F for thighs and drumsticks). (For a gas grill, preheat grill. Reduce heat to medium; adjust for indirect cooking. Grill as above.) Serve chicken with Curry-Cucumber Sauce.

***Curry-Cucumber Sauce:** In a medium bowl, combine 1 cup chopped seeded cucumber, ½ cup mayonnaise or salad dressing, ⅓ cup buttermilk, ½ teaspoon curry powder, and ¼ teaspoon ground ginger. Cover and chill until ready to serve. Makes about 1½ cups.

Nutrition facts per serving: 315 cal., 21 g total fat (5 g sat. fat), 85 mg chol., 421 mg sodium, 3 g carb., 0 g dietary fiber, 26 g protein.

cranberry-maple CHICKEN

Prep: 10 minutes
Grill: 50 minutes
Makes: 4 to 6 servings

½ **cup whole-berry cranberry sauce**

¼ **cup maple syrup**

3 **tablespoons ketchup**

2 **tablespoons cider vinegar**

½ **teaspoon onion powder**

1 **3- to 3½-pound broiler-fryer chicken, halved**

1 For sauce, in a small saucepan combine cranberry sauce, maple syrup, ketchup, vinegar, and onion powder. Bring to boiling; reduce heat. Simmer, uncovered, for 5 minutes, stirring occasionally.

2 For a charcoal grill, arrange medium-hot coals around a drip pan. Test for medium heat above the pan. Place chicken, bone side up, on grill rack over drip pan. Cover and grill for 50 to 60 minutes or until chicken is no longer pink (180°F in thigh), brushing once with sauce during last 10 minutes of grilling. (For a gas grill, preheat grill. Reduce heat to medium; adjust for indirect cooking. Grill as above.)

3 To serve, cut each chicken half into 2 or 3 pieces. Heat remaining sauce until bubbly; serve with chicken.

Nutrition facts per serving: 438 cal., 18 g total fat (5 g sat. fat), 118 mg chol., 274 mg sodium, 31 g carb., 1 g dietary fiber, 37 g protein.

jamaican JERK CHICKEN

Jamaican jerk seasoning is characterized by the use of allspice, thyme, and, of course, peppers. If you have time, marinate for the full 24 hours for the best flavor.

Prep: 30 minutes
Marinate: 8 to 24 hours
Grill: 1 hour
Makes: 4 servings

- 2   3- to 3½-pound broiler-fryer chickens, halved lengthwise
- ½   cup thinly sliced scallions (4)
- ½   cup cider vinegar
- ½   cup orange juice
- ¼   cup soy sauce
- 2   tablespoons olive oil
- 1   tablespoon packed brown sugar
- 1   tablespoon ground allspice
- 1   tablespoon dried thyme, crushed
- 1   small fresh hot red chile pepper, seeded and finely chopped*
- 1   teaspoon cayenne pepper
- 1   teaspoon finely shredded lime zest
- 2   cloves garlic, minced
- ½   teaspoon ground cinnamon
- ½   teaspoon ground nutmeg
- ½   teaspoon ground black pepper

1 Place chicken in a large resealable plastic bag set in a shallow dish. For marinade, in a small bowl combine scallions, vinegar, orange juice, soy sauce, oil, brown sugar, allspice, thyme, chile pepper, cayenne pepper, lime zest, garlic, cinnamon, nutmeg, and black pepper. Pour marinade over chicken. Seal bag; turn to coat chicken. Marinate in the refrigerator for 8 to 24 hours, turning bag occasionally. Drain chicken, reserving marinade.

2 For a charcoal grill, arrange medium-hot coals around a drip pan. Test for medium heat above pan. Place chicken, bone side down, on grill rack over drip pan. Cover and grill for 1 to 1¼ hours or until chicken is no longer pink (180°F in thigh muscle), brushing with reserved marinade halfway through grilling. (For a gas grill, preheat grill. Reduce heat to medium. Adjust for indirect cooking. Grill as above.)

Nutrition facts per serving: 1120 cal., 77 g total fat (21 g sat. fat), 347 mg chol., 1347 mg sodium, 13 g carb., 2 g dietary fiber, 88 g protein.

***Tip:** Because chile peppers contain volatile oils that can burn your skin and eyes, avoid direct contact with them as much as possible. When working with chile peppers, wear plastic or rubber gloves. If your bare hands do touch the peppers, wash your hands and nails well with soap and warm water.

provençal GRILLED CHICKEN AND HERBED PENNE

Prep: 25 minutes
Grill: 12 minutes
Makes: 4 servings

8 ounces dried tomato or garlic-and-herb penne pasta or plain penne pasta

1 pound skinless, boneless chicken breast halves

1 medium zucchini, halved lengthwise

8 thick asparagus spears (8 to 10 ounces total), trimmed

3 tablespoons olive oil

½ teaspoon salt

1 tablespoon snipped fresh thyme

1 tablespoon snipped fresh chives

½ cup finely shredded Asiago cheese (2 ounces; optional)

   Ground black pepper (optional)

1 Cook pasta according to package directions; drain. Return pasta to hot pan and keep warm.

2 Meanwhile, brush chicken, zucchini, and asparagus with 1 tablespoon of the olive oil. Sprinkle all sides of chicken and vegetables with salt.

3 For a charcoal grill, place asparagus on a small piece of foil; place on the rack of an uncovered grill directly over medium coals. Add chicken and zucchini to grill rack; grill for 12 to 15 minutes or until chicken is no longer pink (170°F) and vegetables are tender, turning once halfway through grilling. (For a gas grill, preheat grill. Reduce heat to medium. Place chicken, zucchini, and asparagus on a piece of foil on grill rack over heat. Cover and grill as above.)

4 Transfer chicken and vegetables to a cutting board; cool slightly. Cut chicken and zucchini into 1-inch cubes; cut asparagus into 1-inch pieces. Add chicken, vegetables, the remaining 2 tablespoons olive oil, the thyme, and chives to pasta; toss to combine. If desired, top each serving with cheese and sprinkle with pepper.

Nutrition facts per serving: 441 cal., 13 g total fat (2 g sat. fat), 66 mg chol., 360 mg sodium, 44 g carb., 3 g dietary fiber, 35 g protein.

grilled CHICKEN WITH CUCUMBER-YOGURT SAUCE

Prep: 20 minutes
Grill: 12 minutes
Makes: 4 servings

1   6-ounce carton low-fat
    plain yogurt

¼   cup thinly sliced scallions

2   teaspoons snipped fresh
    mint, or ½ teaspoon
    dried mint, crushed

½   teaspoon ground cumin

¼   teaspoon salt

⅛   teaspoon ground black
    pepper

1   cup chopped, seeded
    cucumber

4   skinless, boneless chicken
    breast halves (1 to
    1¼ pounds total)

⅛   teaspoon ground black
    pepper

    Fresh mint leaves
    (optional)

1 In a medium bowl, combine yogurt, scallions, snipped or dried mint, cumin, salt, and ⅛ teaspoon pepper. Transfer half of the yogurt mixture to a small bowl; set aside. For cucumber-yogurt sauce, stir cucumber into remaining yogurt mixture.

2 Sprinkle chicken breasts with ⅛ teaspoon pepper.

3 For a charcoal grill, place chicken on the rack of an uncovered grill directly over medium coals. Grill for 12 to 15 minutes or until chicken is no longer pink (170°F), turning once halfway through grilling and brushing with reserved yogurt mixture during the last half of grilling. Discard any remaining yogurt mixture. (For a gas grill, preheat grill. Reduce heat to medium. Place chicken on grill rack over heat. Cover and grill as above.)

4 Serve chicken with the cucumber-yogurt sauce. If desired, garnish with fresh mint.

Nutrition facts per serving: 159 cal., 2 g total fat (1 g sat. fat), 68 mg chol., 251 mg sodium, 5 g carb., 0 g dietary fiber, 29 g protein.

grilled lime chicken
WITH WATERMELON SALSA

Prep: 35 minutes
Chill: 1 hour
Grill: 12 minutes
Makes: 6 servings

- 2 **cups chopped seeded watermelon**
- ½ **cup chopped cucumber**
- ½ **cup chopped orange or yellow sweet pepper**
- ½ **of an ear sweet corn, cut from the cob**
- 2 **tablespoons chopped fresh cilantro**
- 1 **to 2 fresh jalapeño chile peppers,* seeded and chopped**
- 1 **tablespoon finely chopped red onion**
- 1 **teaspoon finely shredded lime zest**
- ¼ **cup lime juice**
- 1 **teaspoon packed brown sugar**
- ¼ **teaspoon salt**
- ¼ **teaspoon crushed red pepper**
- 6 **skinless, boneless chicken breast halves**
- 1 **teaspoon lemon-pepper seasoning**
- 1 **tablespoon cooking oil**

1 For salsa, in a medium bowl combine watermelon, cucumber, sweet pepper, corn, cilantro, jalapeño pepper, and onion. In a small bowl, combine ½ teaspoon of the lime zest, 2 tablespoons of the lime juice, brown sugar, salt, and crushed red pepper. Add to watermelon mixture; toss to coat. Cover and chill for 1 hour to let flavors combine.

2 Sprinkle chicken with lemon-pepper seasoning. In a small bowl, combine remaining lime zest, lime juice, and the oil.

3 For a charcoal grill, place chicken on the rack of an uncovered grill directly over medium coals. Grill for 12 to 15 minutes or until chicken is no longer pink (170°F), turning once halfway through grilling and brushing with oil mixture during the last 2 minutes of grilling. (For a gas grill, preheat grill. Reduce heat to medium. Place chicken on grill rack over heat. Cover and grill as above.) Serve chicken with salsa.

Nutrition facts per serving: 221 cal., 4 g total fat (1 g sat. fat), 88 mg chol., 360 mg sodium, 9 g carb., 1 g dietary fiber, 36 g protein.

*Tip: Because chile peppers contain volatile oils that can burn your skin and eyes, avoid direct contact with them as much as possible. When working with chile peppers, wear plastic or rubber gloves. If your bare hands do touch the peppers, wash your hands and nails well with soap and water.

easy MARINATED CHICKEN BREASTS

Prep: 10 minutes
Marinate: 2 to 24 hours
Grill: 12 minutes
Makes: 4 servings

4 small skinless, boneless chicken breast halves (1 to 1¼ pounds total)

¼ cup bottled olive oil and vinegar salad dressing

4 teaspoons reduced-sodium soy sauce

1 tablespoon bottled hoisin sauce

¼ teaspoon ground ginger

1 Place chicken breast halves in a resealable plastic bag set in a deep bowl. For marinade, in a small bowl combine salad dressing, soy sauce, hoisin sauce, and ginger. Pour marinade over chicken. Seal bag; turn to coat chicken. Marinate in the refrigerator for 2 to 24 hours, turning bag occasionally.

2 Drain chicken, discarding marinade. For a charcoal grill, place chicken on the rack of an uncovered grill directly over medium coals. Grill for 12 to 15 minutes or until chicken is no longer pink (170°F). (For a gas grill, preheat grill. Reduce heat to medium. Place chicken on grill rack over heat. Cover and grill as above.)

Nutrition facts per serving: 147 cal., 3 g total fat (1 g sat. fat), 66 mg chol., 147 mg sodium, 1 g carb., 0 g dietary fiber, 26 g protein.

chimichurri CHICKEN

Start to Finish: 20 minutes
Makes: 4 servings

4 skinless, boneless chicken breast halves (about 1¼ pounds total)

3 tablespoons vegetable oil

½ teaspoon salt

¼ teaspoon ground black pepper

12 ounces young green beans

1 tablespoon water

¾ cup packed fresh Italian parsley

1 tablespoon cider vinegar

2 cloves garlic, halved

¼ teaspoon crushed red pepper

1 lemon

❶ Brush chicken with 1 tablespoon of the oil; sprinkle with ¼ teaspoon of the salt and the black pepper.

❷ For a charcoal grill, place chicken on the rack of an uncovered grill directly over medium coals. Grill for 12 to 15 minutes or until no longer pink (170°F), turning once halfway through grilling. (For a gas grill, preheat grill. Reduce heat to medium. Place chicken on rack over heat. Cover; grill as above.)

❸ In a 1½-quart microwave-safe baking dish, combine green beans and the water. Cover with vented plastic wrap. Microwave on 100% power (high) for 3 minutes; drain.

❹ For chimichurri sauce, in a small food processor combine parsley, the remaining 2 tablespoons oil, the vinegar, garlic, the remaining ¼ teaspoon salt, and the crushed red pepper. Cover and process until nearly smooth.

❺ Finely shred zest from the lemon. Cut lemon in half. Serve chicken and green beans with chimichurri sauce. Garnish with lemon zest. Squeeze lemon juice over all.

Nutrition facts per serving: 281 cal., 12 g total fat (2 g sat. fat), 82 mg chol., 376 mg sodium, 8 g carb., 3 g dietary fiber, 35 g protein.

orange CHICKEN KABOBS

Prep: 30 minutes
Marinate: 1 to 4 hours
Grill: 10 minutes
Makes: 8 servings

6 **skinless, boneless chicken breast halves**

½ **teaspoon salt**

¼ **teaspoon ground black pepper**

¾ **cup orange marmalade**

½ **cup chicken broth**

1 **tablespoon finely shredded lemon zest**

¼ **cup lemon juice**

¼ **cup honey**

¼ **cup coarse-grain Dijon-style mustard**

3 **tablespoons light mayonnaise**

1 **tablespoon sesame seeds, toasted**

Sliced scallion (optional)

1 Cut each chicken breast half lengthwise into 4 or 5 strips. Sprinkle chicken with salt and pepper.

2 For marinade, in a medium bowl whisk together orange marmalade, chicken broth, lemon peel, and lemon juice. Add chicken; toss to coat. Cover and marinate in the refrigerator for 1 to 4 hours, stirring occasionally.

3 For dipping sauce, in a small bowl stir together honey, mustard, mayonnaise, and sesame seeds. Cover and chill until ready to serve.

4 Drain chicken, discarding marinade. Thread chicken strips, accordion-style, onto skewers.*

5 For a charcoal grill, grill kabobs on the rack of an uncovered grill directly over medium coals for 10 to 12 minutes or until chicken is no longer pink, turning occasionally to cook evenly. (For a gas grill, preheat grill. Reduce heat to medium. Place kabobs on grill rack over heat. Cover and grill as above.) Serve chicken with dipping sauce. If desired, sprinkle with scallion.

Nutrition facts per 4 ounces cooked chicken plus 2 tablespoons sauce: 224 cal., 4 g total fat (1 g sat. fat), 76 mg chol., 473 mg sodium, 15 g carb., 0 g dietary fiber, 30 g protein.

*Tip: If using wooden skewers, soak them in water for at least 30 minutes before grilling.

chicken WITH PEACH SALSA

Prep: 30 minutes
Marinate: 1 to 4 hours
Grill: 40 minutes
Makes: 4 servings

½ **cup dry white wine**

1½ **teaspoons finely
shredded orange zest**

⅓ **cup orange juice**

2 **tablespoons olive oil or
cooking oil**

1½ **teaspoons snipped fresh
rosemary, or ½ teaspoon
dried rosemary, crushed**

4 **chicken legs (thigh-
drumstick portion)**

2 **medium peaches or
nectarines, or 1⅓ cups
frozen unsweetened
peach slices, thawed**

½ **cup chopped red or green
sweet pepper (1 small)**

1 **ripe avocado, pitted,
peeled, and finely
chopped**

¼ **cup finely chopped
scallion**

2 **tablespoons lime juice**

1 **tablespoon snipped fresh
cilantro**

1 For marinade, in a resealable plastic bag set in a shallow dish, combine wine, orange zest, orange juice, oil, and rosemary. If desired, skin chicken. Add chicken to bag. Seal bag; turn to coat chicken. Marinate in the refrigerator for 1 to 4 hours, turning bag occasionally.

2 Meanwhile, for salsa, peel, pit, and finely chop peaches. In a bowl, combine peaches, sweet pepper, avocado, scallion, lime juice, and cilantro. Cover and chill until ready to serve.

3 Drain chicken, reserving marinade. For a charcoal grill, place chicken, skin side down, on the rack of an uncovered grill directly over medium coals. Grill for 40 to 50 minutes or until chicken is no longer pink (180°F), turning once and brushing with reserved marinade halfway through grilling. Discard any remaining marinade. (For a gas grill, preheat grill. Reduce heat to medium. Place chicken on grill rack over heat. Cover and grill as above.) Serve chicken with salsa.

Nutrition facts per serving: 650 cal., 43 g total fat (10 g sat. fat), 205 mg chol., 166 mg sodium, 13 g carb., 4 g dietary fiber, 47 g protein.

open-face CHICKEN SANDWICHES

Start to Finish: 20 minutes
Makes: 4 servings

- 8 ounces asparagus spears, trimmed
- 2 tablespoons olive oil
  Salt and coarsely ground black pepper
- 4 small skinless, boneless chicken breast halves (1 to 1¼ pounds)
- 4 4-inch portobello mushroom caps, stems removed
- 8 ½-inch-thick slices country Italian bread*
- 1 8-ounce tub cream cheese spread with chive and onion

1 Tear off a 36x18-inch piece of heavy-duty foil; fold in half to make an 18-inch square. Place asparagus in center of foil; drizzle with 1 teaspoon of the oil and sprinkle lightly with salt and pepper. Bring up opposite edges of foil and seal with a double fold. Fold remaining edges to completely enclose asparagus, leaving space for steam to escape. Set aside.

2 Brush chicken and mushrooms with the remaining 5 teaspoons oil; sprinkle lightly with salt and pepper. For a charcoal grill, place chicken, mushrooms, and foil packet with asparagus on the rack of an uncovered grill directly over medium coals. Grill for 12 to 15 minutes or until mushrooms are tender and chicken is no longer pink (170°F), turning chicken and mushrooms once halfway through grilling. (For a gas grill, preheat grill. Reduce heat to medium. Place chicken, mushrooms, and foil packet on grill rack over heat. Cover; grill as above.) Remove chicken, mushrooms, and foil packet from grill; slice mushrooms.

3 Toast bread slices on grill rack for 1 to 2 minutes, turning once. Spread one side of each bread slice with cream cheese.

4 Place a bread slice, cream cheese side up, on each of four serving plates. Top each with a piece of chicken, another bread slice, cream cheese side up, some of the mushrooms, and some of the asparagus.

Nutrition facts per serving: 583 cal., 29 g total fat (15 g sat. fat), 121 mg chol., 751 mg sodium, 40 g carb., 4 g dietary fiber, 37 g protein.

*Tip: If bread slices are too large, use halved slices of bread.

open-face PESTO-CHICKEN BURGERS

Prep: 25 minutes
Grill: 12 minutes
Makes: 4 servings

1 pound ground chicken or ground turkey

4 tablespoons purchased basil pesto

¼ cup finely shredded Parmesan cheese

3 cloves garlic, minced

¼ teaspoon kosher salt or salt

2 3-inch pieces ciabatta bread, or four ¾-inch-thick slices rustic Italian bread

2 tablespoons olive oil

4 slices fresh mozzarella cheese

2 cups fresh basil leaves, arugula, or spring garden mix

8 small tomato slices

Ground black pepper

1 In a medium bowl, combine ground chicken, half of the pesto, the Parmesan, garlic, and salt. Shape into four ½-inch-thick oval patties (to fit bread).

2 Halve ciabatta horizontally. Brush cut side of ciabatta or both sides of Italian bread with olive oil (reserve any extra oil).

3 For a charcoal grill, place patties on greased rack directly over medium coals. Grill, uncovered, for 10 to 13 minutes or until chicken is no longer pink (165°F), turning once halfway through grilling. Top each patty with a mozzarella slice. Cover grill; grill for 1 to 2 minutes more or until cheese is melted. Add bread and grill for 1 to 2 minutes per side or until toasted. (For gas grill, preheat grill. Reduce heat to medium. Place patties on grill rack over heat. Cover; grill as above.)

4 Arrange greens on toasted bread. Top with chicken patties and tomato slices. Stir any remaining olive oil into remaining pesto and drizzle over all. Sprinkle with black pepper.

Nutrition facts per serving: 606 cal., 36 g total fat (9 g sat. fat), 126 mg chol., 902 mg sodium, 35 g carb., 2 g dietary fiber, 236 g protein.

greek-style CHICKEN BURGERS

Prep: 20 minutes
Grill: 14 minutes
Makes: 4 servings

1 **egg white**
⅓ **cup fine dry bread crumbs**
1 **tablespoon milk**
1 **0.7-ounce envelope Italian salad dressing mix (5 teaspoons)**
1 **pound ground chicken or turkey**
4 **pita bread rounds, toasted, or 4 whole wheat hamburger buns, split and toasted**
   Olive-Tomato Relish*
¼ **cup crumbled feta cheese (1 ounce)**

1 In a medium bowl, beat egg white with a whisk; stir in bread crumbs, milk, and half of the salad dressing mix. (Reserve remaining half of salad dressing mix for Olive-Tomato Relish.) Add chicken; mix well. Shape chicken mixture into four ¾-inch-thick patties.

2 For a charcoal grill, grill patties on the rack of an uncovered grill directly over medium coals for 14 to 18 minutes or until no longer pink (165°F), turning once halfway through grilling.

3 Serve the burgers on pita bread rounds with Olive-Tomato Relish and feta cheese.

***Olive-Tomato Relish:** In a small bowl, stir together 2 tablespoons white wine vinegar, 2 teaspoons olive oil, and the remaining half of the dry salad dressing mix. Stir in 1 cup finely chopped tomato, ¼ cup finely chopped cucumber, and ¼ cup finely chopped pitted kalamata olives. Makes about 1⅓ cups.

Nutrition facts per serving: 403 cal., 18 g total fat (5 g sat. fat), 96 mg chol., 1177 mg sodium, 32 g carb., 3 g dietary fiber, 28 g protein.

metric information

The charts on this page provide a guide for converting measurements from the U.S. customary system, which is used throughout this book, to the metric system.

PRODUCT DIFFERENCES

Most of the ingredients called for in the recipes in this book are available in most countries. However, some are known by different names. Here are some common American ingredients and their possible counterparts:

- Sugar (white) is granulated, fine granulated, or castor sugar.
- Powdered sugar is icing sugar.
- All-purpose flour is enriched, bleached, or unbleached white household flour. When self-rising flour is used in place of all-purpose flour in a recipe that calls for leavening, omit the leavening agent (baking soda or baking powder) and salt.
- Light-colored corn syrup is golden syrup.
- Cornstarch is cornflour.
- Baking soda is bicarbonate of soda.
- Vanilla or vanilla extract is vanilla essence.
- Green, red, or yellow sweet peppers are capsicums or bell peppers.
- Golden raisins are sultanas.

VOLUME AND WEIGHT

The United States traditionally uses cup measures for liquid and solid ingredients. The chart, top right, shows the approximate imperial and metric equivalents. If you are accustomed to weighing solid ingredients, the following approximate equivalents will be helpful.

- 1 cup butter, castor sugar, or rice = 8 ounces = $\frac{1}{2}$ pound = 250 grams
- 1 cup flour = 4 ounces = $\frac{1}{4}$ pound = 125 grams
- 1 cup icing sugar = 5 ounces = 150 grams

Canadian and U.S. volume for a cup measure is 8 fluid ounces (237 ml), but the standard metric equivalent is 250 ml.

1 British imperial cup is 10 fluid ounces.

In Australia, 1 tablespoon equals 20 ml, and there are 4 teaspoons in the Australian tablespoon.

Spoon measures are used for smaller amounts of ingredients. Although the size of the tablespoon varies slightly in different countries, for practical purposes and for recipes in this book, a straight substitution is all that's necessary. Measurements made using cups or spoons always should be level unless stated otherwise.

COMMON WEIGHT RANGE REPLACEMENTS

Imperial / U.S.	Metric
$\frac{1}{2}$ ounce	15 g
1 ounce	25 g or 30 g
4 ounces ($\frac{1}{4}$ pound)	115 g or 125 g
8 ounces ($\frac{1}{2}$ pound)	225 g or 250 g
16 ounces (1 pound)	450 g or 500 g
$1\frac{1}{4}$ pounds	625 g
$1\frac{1}{2}$ pounds	750 g
2 pounds or $2\frac{1}{4}$ pounds	1,000 g or 1 Kg

OVEN TEMPERATURE EQUIVALENTS

Fahrenheit Setting	Celsius Setting*	Gas Setting
300°F	150°C	Gas Mark 2 (very low)
325°F	160°C	Gas Mark 3 (low)
350°F	180°C	Gas Mark 4 (moderate)
375°F	190°C	Gas Mark 5 (moderate)
400°F	200°C	Gas Mark 6 (hot)
425°F	220°C	Gas Mark 7 (hot)
450°F	230°C	Gas Mark 8 (very hot)
475°F	240°C	Gas Mark 9 (very hot)
500°F	260°C	Gas Mark 10 (extremely hot)
Broil	Broil	Grill

*Electric and gas ovens may be calibrated using Celsius. However, for an electric oven, increase Celsius setting 10 to 20 degrees when cooking above 160°C. For convection or forced air ovens (gas or electric) lower the temperature setting 25°F/10°C when cooking at all heat levels.

BAKING PAN SIZES

Imperial / U.S.	Metric
9×$1\frac{1}{2}$-inch round cake pan	22- or 23×4-cm (1.5 L)
9×$1\frac{1}{2}$-inch pie plate	22- or 23×4-cm (1 L)
8×8×2-inch square cake pan	20×5-cm (2 L)
9×9×2-inch square cake pan	22- or 23×4.5-cm (2.5 L)
11×7×$1\frac{1}{2}$-inch baking pan	28×17×4-cm (2 L)
2-quart rectangular baking pan	30×19×4.5-cm (3 L)
13×9×2-inch baking pan	34×22×4.5-cm (3.5 L)
15×10×1-inch jelly roll pan	40×25×2-cm
9×5×3-inch loaf pan	23×13×8-cm (2 L)
2-quart casserole	2 L

U.S. / STANDARD METRIC EQUIVALENTS

$\frac{1}{8}$ teaspoon = 0.5 ml	$\frac{1}{3}$ cup = 3 fluid ounces = 75 ml
$\frac{1}{4}$ teaspoon = 1 ml	$\frac{1}{2}$ cup = 4 fluid ounces = 125 ml
$\frac{1}{2}$ teaspoon = 2 ml	$\frac{1}{3}$ cup = 5 fluid ounces = 150 ml
1 teaspoon = 5 ml	$\frac{3}{4}$ cup = 6 fluid ounces = 175 ml
1 tablespoon = 15 ml	1 cup = 8 fluid ounces = 250 ml
2 tablespoons = 25 ml	2 cups = 1 pint = 500 ml
$\frac{1}{4}$ cup = 2 fluid ounces = 50 ml	1 quart = 1 liter

index

Note: Page references in *italics* indicate photographs.